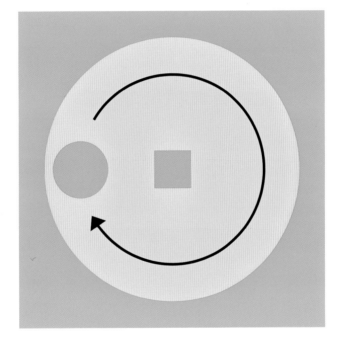

Karakuri - How to Make Mechanical Paper Models That Move
Keisuke Saka

Paper-craft and text	Keisuke Saka
Advisors	Masayuki Kobayashi
	Yasuyuki Shirai
	Toshio Arai
Design	Keisuke Saka, Kohei Masukawa, Eri Hamaji (Redesign/Production)
Translation	Eri Hamaji
Special Thanks	Students at Tama University Hijirigaoka High School, Tokyo, Japan

This book is translated and redesigned from the original book published in Japan:
Keisuke Saka. *Karakuri no Moto: Paper Craft Book*. Tokyo, Japan: Shubunsha, 2007.

Permission to reproduce the Ready to Fly (Climate Change) model granted by Doug Wolske/Noted, LLC.

www.stmartins.com

Library of Congress Cataloging-in-Publication Data

ISBN-13 978-0-312-56669-2

First Edition: March 2010

10 9 8 7 6 5 4 3 2 1

k a r a k u r i

HOW TO MAKE
MECHANICAL PAPER MODELS
THAT MOVE

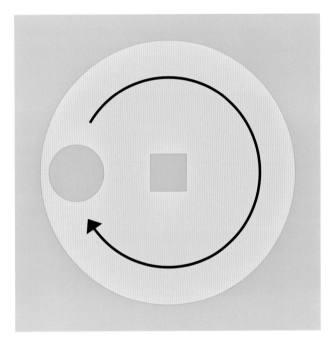

Keisuke Saka
Translated by Eri Hamaji

St. Martins Griffin
New York

How to Use This Book

Make an original karakuri

In Section 1, Karakuri Gallery, you can see some sample karakuri paper crafts made by Keisuke Saka as well as others made by Japanese high school students as a summer project based on the various karakuri diagrams found in this book. Can you imagine how each of them actually moves?

For those of you who want to go ahead and make your own karakuri paper craft without delving into the complicated laws of physics, you can start cutting out a model diagram in Section 4, Basic Karakuri Models, and building it by following the corresponding instructions in Section 3, How to Build Karakuri. When you're done building, try the karakuri by sticking a finger into the hole in the handle and turning it round and round. Then look closely at how the karakuri moves. Does it start to look like something or someone moving? Now it's time for you to get more creative and make your own drawings, cut them out, and paste the parts onto the model to finish up your one-of-a-kind karakuri paper craft!

In Section 5, there are four Fun Karakuri Models designed by Keisuke Saka for you to enjoy building and playing with. They are applications of the simple machines included in Section 4 and work in combination of two or more. Can you tell which mechanisms are used in each toy?

Learn how things work

In Section 2, How Karakuri Work, you will be introduced to the basic logic behind some important karakuri mechanisms. Easy-to-see diagrams help you understand the way they work, and you will also learn that karakuri mechanisms are found in common tools and machines we may use every day without even knowing. The paper-craft models in this book bring the laws of physics behind such items into the 3-D realm.

Those who find the descriptions of karakuri mechanisms in Section 2 to be too wordy and difficult to understand may benefit from first building the models and actually seeing the theories come to life at the turn of a finger. Rereading the explanations after building the model will probably give you a better understanding of how karakuri work.

The 10 Basic Karakuri Models to Assemble

Cam A*

The rod makes a repetitious vertical motion.

INSTRUCTION ▶ p.36
MODEL ▶ p.65

Crank B

The rod sways back and forth by a linkage mechanism.

INSTRUCTION ▶ p.41
MODEL ▶ p.85

Cam B*

Two rods make a vertical movement alternately.

INSTRUCTION ▶ p.37
MODEL ▶ p.69

Crank C

The turning of the crank is converted into a vertical motion.

INSTRUCTION ▶ p.42
MODEL ▶ p.89

Cam C*

The rod makes a repetitious horizontal movement.

INSTRUCTION ▶ p.38
MODEL ▶ p.73

Gear A*

The gear turns horizontally to the handle.

INSTRUCTION ▶ p.43
MODEL ▶ p.93

Cam D*

The rod slides repeatedly in a linear motion.

INSTRUCTION ▶ p.39
MODEL ▶ p.77

Gear B*

The gear turns perpendicularly to the handle.

INSTRUCTION ▶ p.44
MODEL ▶ p.97

Crank A

The rod sways repeatedly in a circular motion.

INSTRUCTION ▶ p.40
MODEL ▶ p.81

Geneva Stop*

A wheel makes turns in a discontinuous rhythm.

INSTRUCTION ▶ p.45
MODEL ▶ p.101

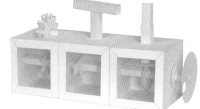

★ These seven karakuri models can be combined to make a model connected with one handle, using the parts on page 105.

The 4 Fun Karakuri Models to Assemble

Tea-Serving Robot

The traditional Japanese tea-serving doll makes a futuristic comeback. Roll the robot forward to serve the tea—be careful; he's a clumsy little thing!

INSTRUCTION ▶ p.46　　　MODEL ▶ p.113

Ready to Fly

A penguin is standing on a glacier and frantically flapping its wings, hoping to fly away. As the body of the penguin moves, the wings sway up and down.

INSTRUCTION ▶ p.48　　　MODEL ▶ p.117

Peek-a-Bear

This friendly-looking bear is actually quite a shy guy. Moving on a crank, he covers his face with his paws but takes a sneak peek at you every few seconds.

INSTRUCTION ▶ p.50　　　MODEL ▶ p.125

Wild Wild West

The tunnel is attached to the base and to the slightly elevated disk at the center. The railroad train moves round while the tunnel and the scenery stand still.

INSTRUCTION ▶ p.52　　　MODEL ▶ p.133

What Is KARAKURI?

"Karakuri" is a Japanese word that means "mechanism." It originally meant all machineries introduced to Japan from China and the West, but in modern times the word often signifies classic dolls and retro toys that move amusingly via simple mechanisms like cams and gears. "Karakuri" can also mean "how things work," or the mysterious workings behind certain things. For example, there are Japanese expressions such as "karakuri of a magic trick" or "karakuri of an incident."

In the middle of the 16th century, the arrival of Portuguese ships introduced the Japanese to intricate Western technologies, such as guns. The Japanese nobles were especially impressed by the clock mechanism, which made a great impact on Japanese craftsmen. In the 17th century, Japan entered a period of isolation during which all cultural and social exchanges with outside countries were completely cut off, a policy that continued until the mid-19th century. These 260 years of isolation were generally peaceful, and most people enjoyed their everyday lives, regardless of social class. This time set the stage for the major technological advancements that lead to the creation of uniquely Japanese karakuri.

One particular characteristic of Japanese karakuri is that they incorporated popular mechanisms not for practical industry or engineering, but for entertainment and amusement, parade floats, theater, and toys. These types of karakuri were enjoyed not only by the upper classes but also by common people. But in order for a toy to be loved and enjoyed every day by common people, it needed to display much more than just accurate movements; a toy also needed fun and playful characteristics to amuse the audience.

One classic karakuri toy that did this was "Chahakobi Ningyo" (illustrated above), which means "tea-serving doll." A doll is carrying a tray on its arms, and when you put a teacup on the tray, the doll moves to the guest being served. When the cup is lifted, the doll stops; after the guest enjoys the tea and places the empty cup on the tray, the doll makes a U-turn and brings the cup back to the server. It was a delightful little toy with a charming act. Another famous karakuri toy is "Yumihiki Douji," which means "bow-bending boy." This doll bends a bow and shoots arrows at a target one after the other, missing the target every few shots or so, which adds to the humor of the action.

During the 18th and 19th centuries, Europe also saw a boom of karakuri-type toys, called automata. Japanese karakuri toys at that time lagged somewhat in terms of precision and materials, due to the long isolation from European influences. On the other hand, these limitations may have been the key factor in the birth and development of Japan's original karakuri, designed with certain restrictions but still imaginative and charming enough to make people smile at a neatly crafted toy.

Karakuri Gallery

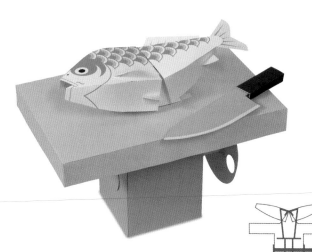

Good Boy!

Lever

This obedient puppy will always sit on your table, waiting for you. Push down his tail, and he will lift his head to reveal a message for the family. You can make your own message card and customize the message.

The Last Resistance

Cam A

Poor fishy struggles at the last moment of its life, before it is turned into delicious pieces of sushi. The up-down movement of two cams at the center of the fish mimics the side flops of a live fish.

Below the Surface

Crank A

Perhaps you never realized that even the most graceful swan frantically paddles its flippers under the water. Two bent cranks are hidden inside the body of this swan to create this movement.

Hesitation

Crank B

He'll never have the courage to test his new flying machine—he keeps holding back at the last moment. That's because a linkage between the toes is fixed to the base and the turning rod of a crank.

Maternal Dilemma

Cam B + Cam C

Mommy's got a dilemma—all of her babies are starving. Which one shall she feed first? The babies move up one after the other on three separate cams, and the mother swivels using two cams on the ends.

Teeter Totter

Cam B

The classic tin-toy robot walks on two feet like a small child. Arms are attached to the top of the rods of the two cams, which is why they move up and down in conjunction with the legs.

Warming Up for Xmas

Cam A

You know everyone is busy just before Christmas, even a reindeer—Noel's getting ready to run a marathon to shed a few pounds. The body moves up and down on a cam, with a coin placed inside as weight.

The Golden Rule

Cam A

These three wise monkeys move by cams of the same shape, but each linkage results in a different movement. You can take them apart individually, change the order, or change the rhythm of each movement.

Walking Beagle — by Meeko

Gear A

The two upper gears mesh with the gears on the base, and each gear works as a crank to move the beagle's legs. The gears are exposed and brightly colored to accent this fun piece.

Thirsty Dinosaur — by Mizuki Noguchi

Gear A

The dinosaur's neck moves up and down to drink from the water pool as the gear turns. What a unique idea to expose the teeth of the gear and turn them into the plates on the back of the stegosaurus!

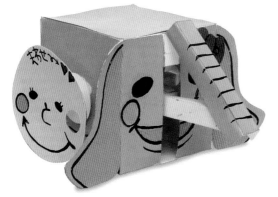

Cutie Elephant — by Sayuri Akagi

Crank B

The rod that moves on a link system becomes the trunk of this cute elephant. Unlike a cam, a crank can still perform the same movement when laid sideways, and this piece does just that.

Come, Come Cat — by Miho Iino

Crank C

This lovely cat entices its prey with a luring paw. Poor thing—the panicky mouse keeps spinning round and round with nowhere to go as the axle holder on the other side of the handle rotates.

Walking a Mad Dog — by Shunsuke

Crank C

The whole base of this piece is the body of the dog. The owner of the dog jitters up and down, while the rampaging dog at the end of the leash masticates violently as the cam on the crank rod turns.

Flying Fish — by Kazuyoshi Mori

Cam B

Fly, fish, fly! This jumping movement may be more easily expressed with a crank, but this piece is cleverly designed as a cam, with the thin bamboo and string working as a link between the two rods of a cam.

Chiming Penguin — by Kaho Fujimaki

Cam C

A musical penguin chimes the bells he holds by flapping his wings. The faster you turn the handle, the more noisily he plays. This special piece is the only one here that incorporates sound.

Dolphin Show — by Rio Kazama

Cam B

Two dolphins take turns jumping out of the water to knock the hanging balls. The waves that hide the rod system and the framework from which the balls hang give this piece a real feeling of a classic toy.

Broken Pedals
by Kana Ariga

Gear A
The two legs of this man are attached to the turning wheel at a slightly off-center spot. The way the ankles, knees, and waist move on a crank gives this piece real humanlike movement.

Serious Sword Fighters
by Shiro B.

Cam D
As the rod goes sideways back and forth, two Japanese sword fighters go to and fro without lifting their heels, keeping a suitable distance between each other. The one who makes the initial move will win.

Hit the Moles!
by Reiko Okuma

Cam B
The moles popping up and the arms trying to hit them are linked to two rods inside that move up and down alternately. The intricate mechanism inside is unimaginable from the piece's comical appearance.

Yes, You Can Do It!
by Shiori

Geneva Stop
For every full turn of the handle, only $\frac{1}{6}$ of the wheel turns, pushing up the feet of a girl on a horizontal bar. The irregular movement shows her strenuous physical effort, though she never makes it over.

It's Time for a Break!   by T. Ishida

Cam D

Cuckoos pop out of the clock to let you know it's three o'clock. The lower one pops out from the display stand itself, using the movement of the frame inside. The way the doors close on a string is also very smart.

A Day in Japan   by S.W.

Geneva Stop

The sun and moon alternately overlook Mount Fuji. They pop up as they hit the tips of the wheel inside, and then disappear again. The irregular movement of the solar bodies represents a day in fast motion.

Kite in the Dusk   by Ririko Fujishima

Crank A

This is a very poetic piece. A boy flies a kite, standing in a field and reaching his arm up high. As the kite sways back and forth in the orange sky, you might find yourself reminiscing about memories of childhood.

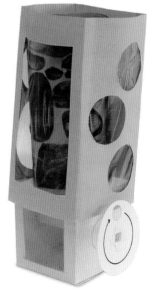

Fish in the Ocean   by Marie Ueda

Gear B

Images of various fish are collaged on a cylinder attached to a horizontal gear. Looking through the windows fixed on the display stand, it feels as if you're on an excursion to an aquarium.

A Pirate Ship   by Sachi Otomo

Crank A	A ship of brave pirates navigates through the stormy sea as it wildly sways on a crank. A wooden stick is put through the rod (also used as the ship's mast) to strengthen the rod and the display stand of this piece.

Boat's in Danger!   by Satomi Sakurai

Crank B	A rowboat is nearly overturned by the large wave, but the man rides it out every time. The inside of the display stand is painted to resemble deep ocean, and the cellophane is a clever expression of the crashing wave.

Space-Traveler Bicycle   by Hashimoto

Geneva Stop	A bicycle made of wire turns its pedals as tips of a Geneva stop hit the central disk. As the pedals irregularly turn, it amost looks as if an invisible man is in the empty seat, trying to move this heavy bicycle forward.

Old Sewing Machine   by Aya Okada

Cam A	You can hear the click-clock as the needle moves up and down on a cam and the fabric slides forward using the rotation of the bearing inside. A very nice use of zigzagged cardboard causes more friction.

Wandering in the Sky

by Tetsuya Ito & P. Crafter

Cam B

Here, two cams with separate handles are attached next to each other. As the two handles are turned simultaneously, the red dragon begins to wander about high up in the sky, right above the cotton clouds.

Karakuri Dragon

by Fujiwara

Cam B

The dragon moves its horns up and down and chomps its mouth as the upper jaw is pushed down inside the display stand. With a handle as the ear, this piece takes full advantage of one karakuri mechanism.

Karakuri Alien

by Maccin DaVinci

Cam A

Just by looking at this, you may guess that the rocket will simply pop up, but that's not all—the lips of the alien move, too! Parts of a plastic bottle and film-case lids give this piece an alienlike texture.

I'm a Hungry Snake!

by Erina Suzuki

Crank B

This snake looks like it's either raising its head and sticking out its tongue or widely opening its jaws. The camouflage pattern adds to the peculiar and mysterious feeling of this piece.

Uppercut!
by Hayato Mori

Crank C

The glove attached to the rod hits the opponent's jaw, throwing a perfect uppercut. Just look at the guy's face—ouch!

Guitarist
by Shota Fujimori

Cam B

A thumbtack is used to transmit the rods' movement to the hand striking the guitar strings. Notice—it's a Gibson Firebird!

A Kettle
by Okuyo Yokokawa

Crank C

No matter how far the kettle is tilted, not a drop pours out—it's all in vain. Its being so nicely crafted adds to the humor.

Tell Us Your Opinion!
by Shimodori

Cam B

This guy won't back off with the mic until you speak. The arm could have been moved to the side, but it's funnier this way.

I'll Keep Running Forever
by T.S.

Crank C

The smiling runner jumps over the obstacle on the disk attached to the bearing inside—he just barely makes it!

An Angry Person
by Ayaka Tomozumi

Cam B

This person is so angry with you he won't stop punching at you, but the slowness of his fist just makes you want to laugh.

How Karakuri Work

Lever

A lever is one of the oldest mechanisms invented by humans. A lever is a simple machine that can multiply an applied mechanical force or change the direction of a force. Levers tend to go unnoticed because the mechanism is commonly used in almost every tool and machine.

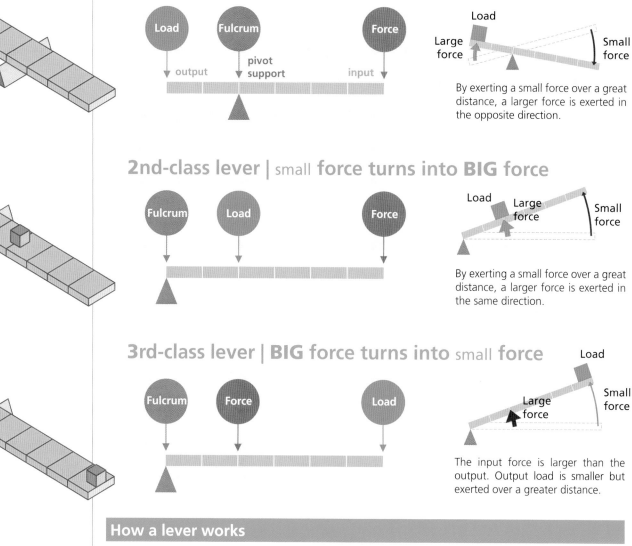

1st-class lever | small **force turns into BIG** force

Load   Fulcrum   Force

output   pivot support   input

By exerting a small force over a great distance, a larger force is exerted in the opposite direction.

2nd-class lever | small **force turns into BIG** force

Fulcrum   Load   Force

Load   Large force   Small force

By exerting a small force over a great distance, a larger force is exerted in the same direction.

3rd-class lever | **BIG** force turns into small **force**

Fulcrum   Force   Load

Load   Large force   Small force

The input force is larger than the output. Output load is smaller but exerted over a greater distance.

How a lever works

When you're lifting a load, there is a law of physics in the relationship of the distance between the fulcrum and the force and the amount of the applied force. The longer the distance, the less force is needed. For example, if you the double the distance, the force decreases to $\frac{1}{2}$, and triple the distance, the force decreases to $\frac{1}{3}$, and so on. This is called the "lever mechanism." But if you want to lift the weight to the same height, the force must be applied over a greater distance—double, or maybe triple.

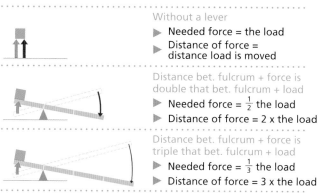

Without a lever
- ▶ Needed force = the load
- ▶ Distance of force = distance load is moved

Distance bet. fulcrum + force is double that bet. fulcrum + load
- ▶ Needed force = $\frac{1}{2}$ the load
- ▶ Distance of force = 2 x the load

Distance bet. fulcrum + force is triple that bet. fulcrum + load
- ▶ Needed force = $\frac{1}{3}$ the load
- ▶ Distance of force = 3 x the load

Let's make it & try!

A lever karakuri model is not included in this book. But the handles of all the models use a wheel axle, which is a variation of a lever. Look for this and other functions in the models that use the lever mechanism to change the size or direction of a force.

Lever and wheel axle

A wheel axle is a set of two wheels of different sizes that rotate on the same axle. If you think of the axle as the fulcrum and the edges of the wheels as load and force, you can see that this is actually a 2nd-class lever. The steering wheel of a car, the grip of a screwdriver, and the handle of a faucet are some examples of this type of lever. By using the lever mechanism, the wheel axle can turn a central axle that is otherwise difficult to turn.

Rotating axle (Fulcrum)

Wheel that does the work (Load)

Wheel on which force is applied (Force)

Pliers

Crowbar

Fulcrum

Fulcrum

Piano

Inside a piano, the force applied from the fingers hitting the keys is transmitted through a number of levers and lifts the felt-tipped hammers, which hit the strings to make beautiful sounds. The same force goes through a different lever to release the damper that is pressed against the strings. The pipe organ and electric piano work differently, of course.

string   damper   hammer   keyboard

Bottle opener

Fulcrum

Hand-press juicer

Fulcrum

Nail clippers

Fulcrum

2nd-class lever

3rd-class lever

Fulcrum

Nail clippers are a combination of two different levers. The upper lever multiplies the force from the finger and transmits it to the sharp-edged lower lever. Because the distance between the force and the load on the lower lever is very close, not that much force is required to move the load. This is why you can cut through a hard, thick nail with just a gentle push of your fingertip.

Cake tongs

Fulcrum

In order to hold a delicate cake slice without smushing it, the levers open widely to lessen the applied force.

Scale

Scale display

Weight lever

Spring

Force

Fulcrum

Load

Spring   Rack & Pinion (see p.26)   Linkage (see p.28)

A scale measures weight by using the spring's ability to stretch. But instead of using a spring that can hold hundreds of pounds of human weight, a scale uses a 3rd-class lever to change weight into a force much smaller that small springs can hold. When the springs stretch, the weight lever goes down, and then the force goes through a linkage and a gear to rotate the scale display. A scale is made up of four of these levers, so that weight can be measured accurately by standing on its center.

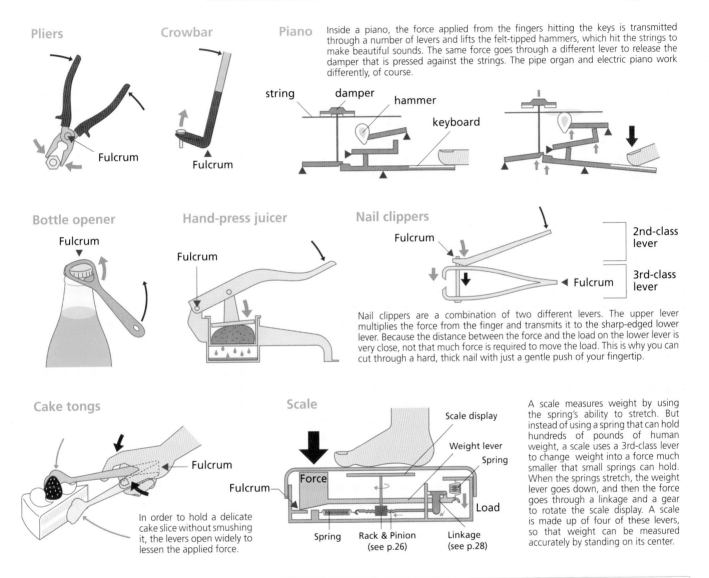

Could Archimedes Lift the Planet Earth?

Archimedes was a Greek scientist who lived in the 3rd century B.C. and designed many machines and weapons people at that time used. He was the one who first defined the laws of the lever, though the lever mechanism had been used in practice for some time. One of his famous quotes is "Give me a place to stand and I will move the earth!"

But could earth really be lifted by a lever? If so, how long would it need to be? Well, let's think of the moon as fulcrum and the sun as force. The distance between earth and moon is 237,700 miles, about 400 times more than the distance between earth and sun, so the force needed is only $\frac{1}{400}$ of earth's weight. The weight of the earth is approximately 6 trillion tons (6 with 21 zeros after it—can you imagine?), so even $\frac{1}{400}$ of that is a lot: 15 with 18 zeros after it. Even if the handle of the lever could be stretched to the far end of the universe, you would still need thousands of tons of force to lift the earth. So even Archimedes may not have been able to lift the earth, after all.

Cam

A cam is a mechanism that turns or moves variously shaped disks in order to change the direction or rhythm of how parts move along the contour of those disks.

It is used in many machines to make intricate movements with fewer parts, just by changing the shape of the disk.

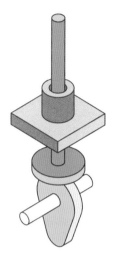

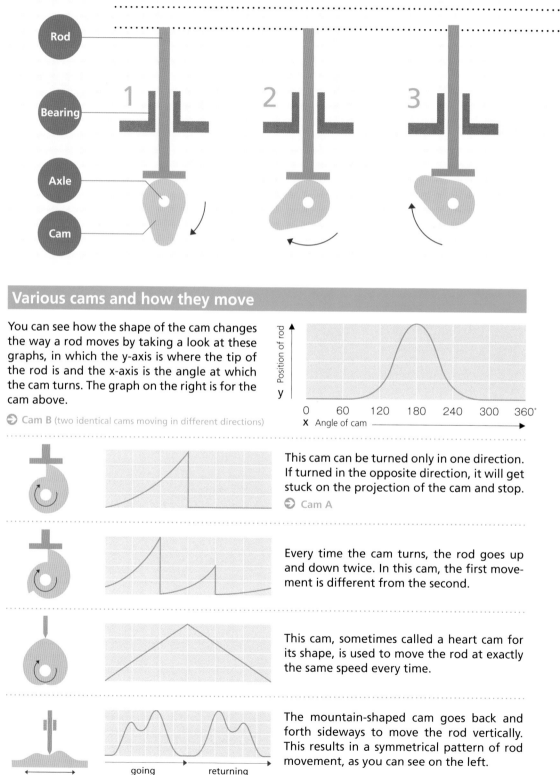

Rod

Bearing

Axle

Cam

1   2   3

Various cams and how they move

You can see how the shape of the cam changes the way a rod moves by taking a look at these graphs, in which the y-axis is where the tip of the rod is and the x-axis is the angle at which the cam turns. The graph on the right is for the cam above.

y Position of rod

0   60   120   180   240   300   360°
x Angle of cam

➲ Cam B (two identical cams moving in different directions)

This cam can be turned only in one direction. If turned in the opposite direction, it will get stuck on the projection of the cam and stop.
➲ Cam A

Every time the cam turns, the rod goes up and down twice. In this cam, the first movement is different from the second.

This cam, sometimes called a heart cam for its shape, is used to move the rod at exactly the same speed every time.

going   returning

The mountain-shaped cam goes back and forth sideways to move the rod vertically. This results in a symmetrical pattern of rod movement, as you can see on the left.

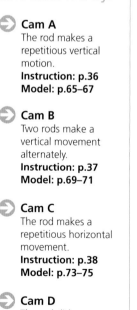

Let's make it & try!

➲ **Cam A**
The rod makes a repetitive vertical motion.
Instruction: p.36
Model: p.65–67

➲ **Cam B**
Two rods make a vertical movement alternately.
Instruction: p.37
Model: p.69–71

➲ **Cam C**
The rod makes a repetitious horizontal movement.
Instruction: p.38
Model: p.73–75

➲ **Cam D**
The rod slides repeatedly in a linear motion.
Instruction: p.39
Model: p.77–79

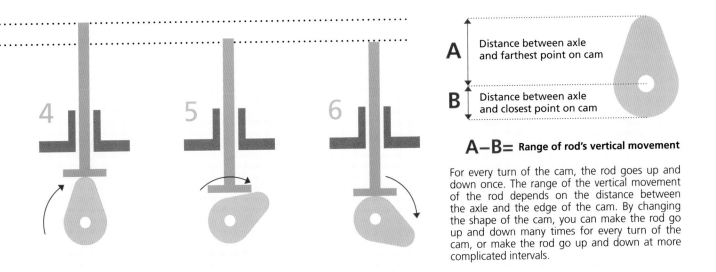

A Distance between axle and farthest point on cam

B Distance between axle and closest point on cam

A−B= Range of rod's vertical movement

For every turn of the cam, the rod goes up and down once. The range of the vertical movement of the rod depends on the distance between the axle and the edge of the cam. By changing the shape of the cam, you can make the rod go up and down many times for every turn of the cam, or make the rod go up and down at more complicated intervals.

Where cams are used

Pinspotter

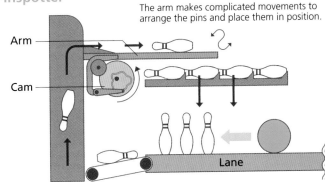

The arm makes complicated movements to arrange the pins and place them in position.

Arm

Cam

Lane

A pinspotter is a very important machine at any bowling alley, collecting all the pins hit by the ball and rearranging them for the next set. Inside the pinspotter, there is actually a cam, on a very intricate guide rail. An arm that corresponds to the movement of the cam goes up, down, left, and right to arrange the 10 pins in the right spot every time. This complicated machine, which has other functions such as collecting the balls and pins remaining on the lane, was invented in the USA about 60 years ago, and its invention made bowling explosively popular. Before pinspotters came about, there were "pinboys" in every alley who would pick up all the pins and rearrange them by hand.

Knitting machine or loom

A knitting machine works by using a number of needles to catch yarn to knit into a fabric; a cam is used to do that. The cam is placed inside a carriage device and set on a row of horizontally aligned needles. Every time the cam touches the projection on the needles, the needles are automatically pushed out one after the other. Back in the days before computers, looms had specially designed cylinders with projections at the tip of the needles that turned to select only the needles that corresponded to a particular carriage, which is how patterns were made. This is also a variation of a cam.

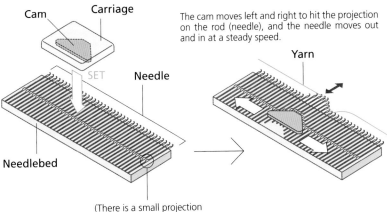

Cam

Carriage

The cam moves left and right to hit the projection on the rod (needle), and the needle moves out and in at a steady speed.

Yarn

SET

Needle

Needlebed

(There is a small projection in the middle of the rod.)

Crank

A crank is a mechanism that uses a hook-shaped axle
to convert a rotation into a linear motion,
or, vice versa, a linear motion into a rotation.
By combining a crank with a linkage,
a very complicated motion can be produced.

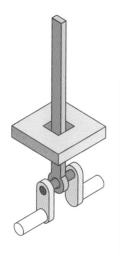

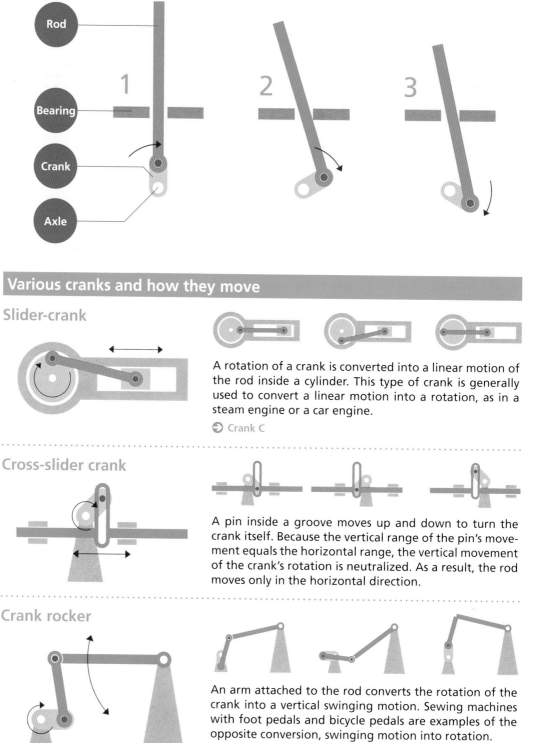

Rod

Bearing

Crank

Axle

1

2

3

Various cranks and how they move

Slider-crank

A rotation of a crank is converted into a linear motion of the rod inside a cylinder. This type of crank is generally used to convert a linear motion into a rotation, as in a steam engine or a car engine.

→ Crank C

Cross-slider crank

A pin inside a groove moves up and down to turn the crank itself. Because the vertical range of the pin's movement equals the horizontal range, the vertical movement of the crank's rotation is neutralized. As a result, the rod moves only in the horizontal direction.

Crank rocker

An arm attached to the rod converts the rotation of the crank into a vertical swinging motion. Sewing machines with foot pedals and bicycle pedals are examples of the opposite conversion, swinging motion into rotation.

→ Crank B

Let's make it & try!

→ **Crank A**
The rod sways repeatedly in a circular motion.
Instruction: **p.40**
Model: **p.81–83**

→ **Crank B**
The rod sways back and forth by a linkage mechanism.
Instruction: **p.41**
Model: **p.85–87**

→ **Crank C**
Turns of a crank is converted into a vertical motion.
Instruction: **p.42**
Model: **p.89–91**

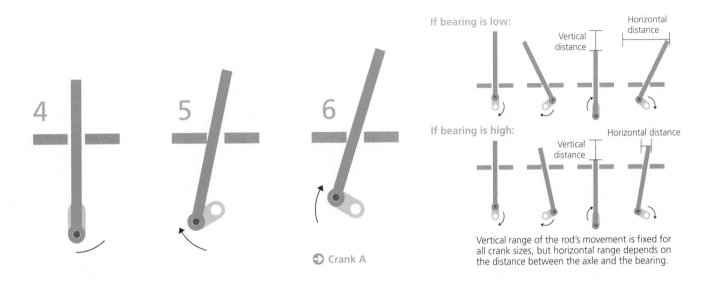

If bearing is low:

Vertical distance

Horizontal distance

If bearing is high:

Vertical distance

Horizontal distance

↻ Crank A

Vertical range of the rod's movement is fixed for all crank sizes, but horizontal range depends on the distance between the axle and the bearing.

Where cranks are often used

Internal Combustion Engine

A car is one of the most commonly used machines in our daily lives, and its internal combustion engine uses various mechanisms, including cam and crank. The engine usually works in a four-stroke cycle, also known as an Otto cycle: intake, compression, power, and exhaust. In one full four-stroke cycle, the crank and the piston make a full movement twice, of rotation and linear motion, respectively.

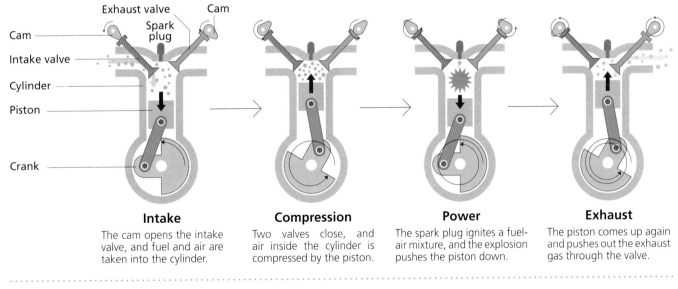

Cam — Exhaust valve — Spark plug

Cam — Intake valve — Cylinder — Piston — Crank

Intake
The cam opens the intake valve, and fuel and air are taken into the cylinder.

Compression
Two valves close, and air inside the cylinder is compressed by the piston.

Power
The spark plug ignites a fuel-air mixture, and the explosion pushes the piston down.

Exhaust
The piston comes up again and pushes out the exhaust gas through the valve.

Electric toothbrush

For those types where the brush rotates at the tip, the rotation of the motor converts to the rotation of the brush using two cranks. Small gears at the tip of the motor, called pinion, or crown gear, function the same way as the bevel gear on p.26, converting the rotation into a third dimension.

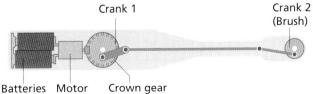

Crank 1

Crank 2 (Brush)

Batteries Motor Crown gear

Gear

A gear is a mechanism used in things we all know,
such as a watch or a bicycle. It can change the direction
of rotation, as well as the speed and amount of force.
Gears can engage with not only other gears,
but also a chain or a belt to exert force over a distance.

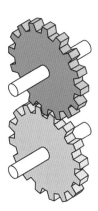

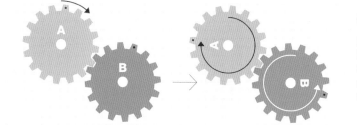

Gears of the same size

If two gears have the same number of teeth, gear B makes one rotation for every rotation of gear A. The speed of the gears is the same—only the direction changes.

BIG gear & small gear

If gear A has half the number of teeth as gear B, B rotates only half a cycle with a full rotation of A, so the speed is also reduced by half.

➔ Gear A

Various gears and how they move

The gear above left is called "spur gear" and is probably the most common type. There are other kinds of gears used in machines, made in various shapes and engaged in various ways.

Bevel gear

In this type of gear, two conically shaped gears intersect perpendicularly or at an angle to each other. This mechanism can convert a two-dimensional rotation into a three-dimensional motion.

➔ Gear B (This mechanism is used for regular gears engaged at a 90° angle.)

Worm gear

By turning an axle with screwlike grooves, the gear is turned very slowly (one tooth every time the axle turns). This gear is used to quickly slow down the high-speed rotation of a motor. It got its name because the rotating axle looks like a crawling worm.

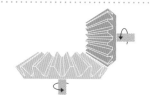

Rack and pinion

A small gear (pinion) engages the teeth on a flat bar (rack) that moves in a linear motion. Vice versa, the pinion can be rotated by moving the rack. This mechanism is used in camera tripods.

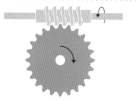

Planetary gear (or sun and planet gear)

The axles of two gears of different sizes have been attached by a free-moving arm, resembling a planet (small gear) orbiting around the sun (large gear). This unique mechanism makes a complicated movement of rotation and revolution, used in amusement-park teacup rides and wall-mounted pencil sharpeners.

Let's make it & try!

➔ **Gear A**
The gear turns horizontally to the handle.
Instruction: p.43
Model: p.93–95

➔ **Gear B**
The gear turns perpendicularly to the handle.
Instruction: p.44
Model: p.97–99

Gear and pulley

The angle or direction of gear rotation can be changed by using a belt made of materials like rubber instead of a chain. The gears on top are engaged by a criss-crossed belt, and the ones below are engaged by a belt turned sideways. Belts cannot be placed directly on gears, so various adjustments are made to gears used in real machines in order to keep the belt from slipping off the gears.

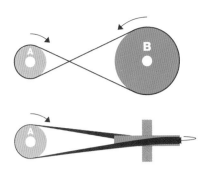

Multiple gears

If a small gear C is placed between A and B, the direction of B stays the same as A. Gears A and B in the left picture have the same number of teeth, so the speed of A and B are the same, regardless of the number of teeth of C, but the direction and speed of rotation can be readily changed by engaging a number of gears of different sizes.

Paired with a large gear
Pedals are *light*, but gear moves slowly.

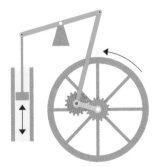

Paired with a small gear
Pedals are *heavy*, but gear moves fast.

Gear and chain

If the axles of two gears are far apart, they can be engaged using a chain. A bicycle is a known example of this. How the gears are engaged influences the required force and speed of the pedals, so the speed of the bicycle changes depending on the gear, even if you apply the same force.

Where gears are also used

Bicycle bells

You've probably seen those bicycle bells that ring when you pull a little lever. Inside, there are four gears of various sizes. When the lever is pulled, it is automatically pushed back by a spring, and one full movement of the lever is magnified by the gears into several rotations of a bar on top with metal on each end, which strikes the bell to make a loud ringing sound.

Spring

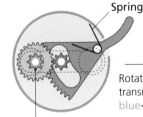

Rotation of gear is transmitted in the order of blue-green-yellow-pink.

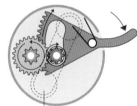

The green gear is underneath the yellow and meshes with the blue.

There is a bar with two metal ends that rotates on the same axle as the pink gear.

Is Pride the Mother of Invention? The Planetary Gear of James Watt

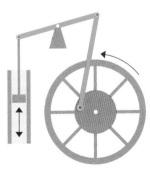

Watt's design of the planetary gear that converts the piston's linear motion into rotation.

It would have been much easier to make it with a crank, as you can see above.

James Watt (1736–1819) was an inventor who first came up with a working steam engine that greatly contributed to the Industrial Revolution. He is also known as the inventor of the planetary gear, which he designed to convert the vertical motion in the steam-engine cylinder into a circular motion that could be used in factories.

There's an interesting episode behind the invention of the planetary gear. At first, Watt's design was based on a crank mechanism commonly used at the time. But one day, an engineer who was working for Watt had too much to drink at a pub and blurted out all the secrets of their new project. When a factory owner who was at the pub heard it, he stole the idea and got it patented! Watt didn't want to pay the patent fee to use his own invention, so he decided to create an entirely new mechanism, the planetary gear.

Years later when the patent expired, most internal engines were changed to a crank mechanism, but various forms of the planetary gear are still used in many machines and tools today.

Linkage

By adding a few arms to link simple devices, combinations of linear and circular motion can be turned into various complicated movements. Such a mechanism is called a linkage, and most machines we use are made up of linkages.

Four-joint composition of basic linkage

The image on the left represents the most basic form of linkage. Four arms are linked by four rotating joints, with only the pink arm on the bottom in a fixed position. If you rotate the yellow handle, the green and blue arms always make the same movements. These motions can be used in various tools and machines.

By changing the lengths of the arms or the motion of the joints, intricate movements can be created to suit the purpose of many machines. Linkages on the right page are made of the same four arms, but they make different movements depending on which arm is fixed in position.

Fixed position

1   2   3   4

Where linkages are often used

Power shovel

By pushing the joint of arm A and arm B, arm C moves down. Because C is shorter than A, C swings down farther than A, which is how the shovel digs up dirt from the ground. Because a very large force is needed to do this, an oil-hydraulic pressure system is used, in which oil is poured into a cylinder to push the rod down.

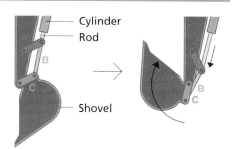

Cylinder
Rod
Shovel

Steering system of a car

The rotation of the handle is transmitted through a rack and pinion gear (see p.26) to arm A (tie rod). As A is moved to the left or right, arms C (knuckle arms) attached to the tires correspond in a circular motion. By making A shorter than D, the two tires tilt at different angles, which allows the car to turn street corners smoothly.

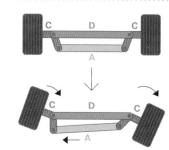

Umbrella

A linkage mechanism is used to open and close this common tool everyone uses. The image on the right is the most simple type of an umbrella mechanism. In an automatic umbrella (one that opens with a button) or a compact umbrella, another linkage connects to this basic linkage. If you happen to have an umbrella at home, take a look at it yourself.

Let's make it & try!

Crank B
The linkage makes a rod sway back and forth.
Instruction: p.41
Model: p.89–91

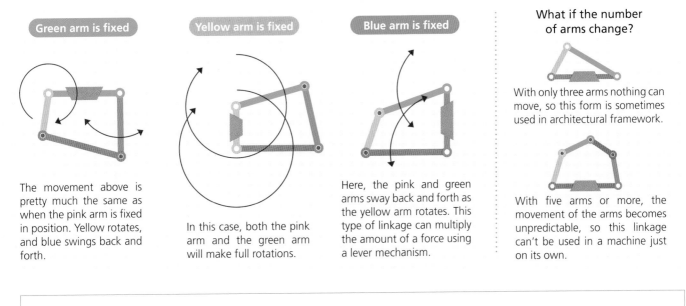

Green arm is fixed

The movement above is pretty much the same as when the pink arm is fixed in position. Yellow rotates, and blue swings back and forth.

Yellow arm is fixed

In this case, both the pink arm and the green arm will make full rotations.

Blue arm is fixed

Here, the pink and green arms sway back and forth as the yellow arm rotates. This type of linkage can multiply the amount of a force using a lever mechanism.

What if the number of arms change?

With only three arms nothing can move, so this form is sometimes used in architectural framework.

With five arms or more, the movement of the arms becomes unpredictable, so this linkage can't be used in a machine just on its own.

Karakuri inside a toilet tank—can't live without it!

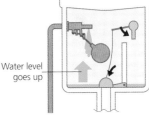

Water-storing functions

Ball tap (or ball cock)

Float ball
lighter than water

Tank fill tube

Flush valve
heavier than water

Flush tube

Tank lever

Chain

Overflow tube
This tube sucks up all water that comes above it, keeping the tank from overflowing.

Flush functions

Water level goes down

When the tank lever is pulled, the flush valve is lifted and water goes down the flush tube. The ball tap brings new water into the tank as the float ball sinks, but water drains so fast the water level goes down.

Water level goes up

When the tank is nearly empty, the flush valve falls with its own weight, closing up the flush tube. As the water level starts to go up, the float ball closes the ball tap, stopping the flow of water into the tank.

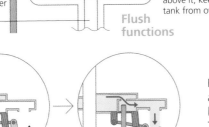

Inside the ball tap
As the rod attached to the float ball moves up and down, the valve inside the ball tap opens and closes. From this image with colored parts, you can see that the ball tap is a four-joint linkage mechanism.

Did you know that the history of the flush-toilet system goes back quite a long time? Archaeologists have found 4,000-year-old ruins on the island of Crete that had flush-toilet systems with drainage and even a seat! The flush toilet we use today with chains and levers to release water from the tank was invented in late-19th–century England. Though invented during the time when there was not even electricity, the same basic mechanism is still used today, with some improvements and variations.

The force of the finger on the lever engages various linkages and laws of buoyancy and gravity to flush out and fill up the tank at once. So next time your tank becomes broken, perhaps you can try fixing it yourself—just remember to stop the tank fill tube first!

Geneva Stop

A Geneva stop is a mechanism that converts a continuous rotation into a rotation that stops every now and then. It was given the name of the Swiss city of watchmakers, where it was first applied to springs inside watches; a mechanism similar to this is used in film projectors.

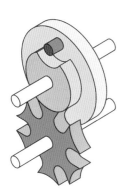

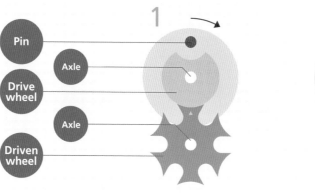

Pin

Axle

Drive wheel

Axle

Driven wheel

A drive wheel with a crescent-shaped cutout begins to rotate. The "fin" of the driven wheel is aligned with the drive wheel.

The driven wheel remains stationary as the drive wheel rotates further.

Various mechanisms that produce intermittent motions

A repeated pattern of motion that moves, stops, and moves again is called intermittent motion. In order to produce intermittent rotary motions from the continuous rotations in most motors, a variety of mechanisms are invented using gears and cams, including the Geneva stop above.

Intermittent motion with gears

The yellow gear rotates continuously, but the blue gear stays still when teeth are not meshed. On the left, blue turns $\frac{1}{10}$ of the way for every rotation of yellow, and on the right, blue turns $\frac{1}{4}$ for every rotation of yellow.
Various intermittent motions are produced by changing the number or pattern of the teeth.

Intermittent motion with cams

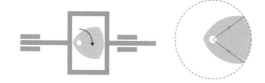

A cam rotating inside a frame moves a rod sideways. One edge of the cam is equal to the circumference of an imaginary circle drawn around the central axle, so when this edge is not touching the frame while the cam is moving, the rod stays still.

Escapement

As the yellow gear tries to rotate, it hits the hooks on the swinging blue arm. The gear rotates while the left hook is disengaged, but when the next tooth hits the hook on the right it turns the other way, and so the oscillation is repeated. This mechanism is used in pendulum clocks and mechanical watches.

Let's make it & try!

➜ **Geneva stop**
The wheel turns in a discontinuous rhythm.
Instruction: p.45
Model: p.101-103

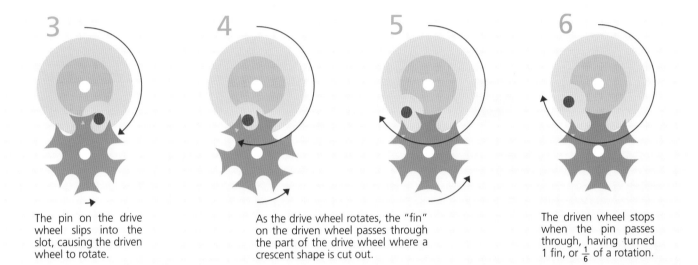

3 The pin on the drive wheel slips into the slot, causing the driven wheel to rotate.

4 As the drive wheel rotates, the "fin" on the driven wheel passes through the part of the drive wheel where a crescent shape is cut out.

5

6 The driven wheel stops when the pin passes through, having turned 1 fin, or $\frac{1}{6}$ of a rotation.

Where intermittent rotary motion is often used

Film projector

Movies work in the same way as flip-book animation. The film is advanced frame by frame, and each frame is slightly different from the last so that the human eye sees it in motion. The film looks like it's moving continuously, but it's actually in intermittent motion. Each frame stands still in front of the lens for a fraction of a second and is projected on the screen before the light is shut off and the film is advanced to the next frame.

The mechanism that makes this happen is called the Maltese cross, a combination of two wheels, one with a pin (yellow wheel) and another in a cross shape (blue wheel). The yellow wheel continuously rotates via a motor, but the blue rotates only when the pin enters one of its slots and another gear on the same axle, called a sprocket (pink wheel), turns the film to the next frame. When the pin leaves, the cross stops turning and the shutter opens up to project the film onto the screen.

In a regular film or animation, 24 frames are projected each second. That means each frame stops in front of the lamp only for less than $\frac{1}{24}$ of a second (In the Maltese cross on the right, $\frac{1}{4}$ of the motor's rotation is used to move the frame, and it stays still for the remaining $\frac{3}{4}$ of the rotation, which actually makes it $\frac{1}{32}$ of a second.) At this fast speed, the human eye cannot detect the intermittence, so it just looks as if the film is continuously flowing and the picture is moving on screen.

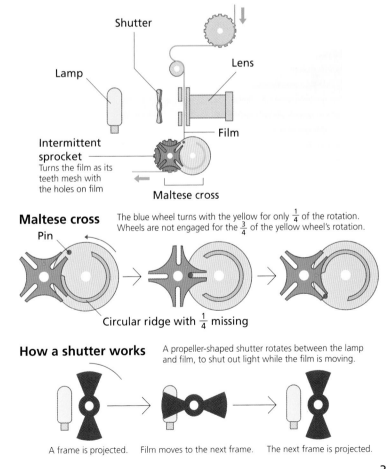

Shutter

Lamp

Lens

Film

Intermittent sprocket
Turns the film as its teeth mesh with the holes on film

Maltese cross

Maltese cross The blue wheel turns with the yellow for only $\frac{1}{4}$ of the rotation. Wheels are not engaged for the $\frac{3}{4}$ of the yellow wheel's rotation.

Pin

Circular ridge with $\frac{1}{4}$ missing

How a shutter works A propeller-shaped shutter rotates between the lamp and film, to shut out light while the film is moving.

A frame is projected.   Film moves to the next frame.   The next frame is projected.

The World of Creation

Have you ever counted how many objects or tools you use every day yet you don't really know how they work? There are so many! If you stop for a moment and take a close look at the tool or device you're using, you may find yourself asking questions like "How does this work?" or "When was this invented?" Then, all of a sudden, you'll see that the world around you is much more interesting than you ever thought, full of things to discover and learn.

Basic Elements of a Machine

If you open a tool or device to see what's inside, it looks really complicated all together. But each of the parts inside is made up of simple and basic mechanisms, like lever, crank, cam, gear, and linkage. A lever is actually nothing but a long stick, but if it's used in the right way it turns into a "magic wand" that can change the amount or direction of force. Levers were invented a long time ago—they were used to move stones for building Egyptian pyramids—and the same simple mechanism is used to this day.

Working Together With Electronics

Our predecessors spent a lot of time using their imagination to make life more convenient and comfortable, improving upon simple mechanisms in order to invent new machines. During the past century, there have been extraordinary developments in mechanical and electronic technology that now enables us to send humans to outer space and use robots to assist our lives.

Important Part of Our Future

No matter how advanced we become in electronic technology, there is, however, no doubt that simple and basic mechanisms will continue to play an important role. I say this because a machine can make a certain movement only with the application of an outside force—whether it be human power, motor, or engine—and mechanisms are needed to convert and transmit that force from the source to the machine.

New Creation

The more you try to perfect your skills in something, the more you realize that the basic foundation is the most important. Likewise, when you are trying to design something new, knowing these simple mechanisms will help you to make a machine that is more original, more useful, and easier to use than anything that existed before. It will also help you transmit your creativity from your head to your fingers to draw, cut, and paste, which liberates your mind and leads to new ideas full of creativity.

So how would you like to take a trip back in time to feel the passion of ancient inventors, taking each of the simple machines—lever, crank, cam, gear, and linkage—and putting them together through trial and error, like pieces of a jigsaw puzzle? This book is a good place to start your trip, and it will even take you to the future, to a new world of creation full of dreams and imagination.

Toshio Arai
Currently CEO, Concept Plus Co., Ltd.
Previously worked at Sony as a technical engineer for 27 years
Important figure in the development of the Walkman and Discman

How to Build Karakuri

Seven of the ten basic karakuri models included in this book (Cam A, Cam B, Cam C, Cam D, Gear A, Gear B, and Geneva stop) can make a model that's connected with one handle. If you want to build the kits connectedly, please see p.105 before you start.

Basic Paper Crafting Techniques

One great thing about paper crafting is that you can somehow manage without special tools or skills. But with the right tools and helpful hints, you can make the process much easier and also improve the result.
So before you start, let's gather the needed tools and learn some tips.
Keep in mind when you're working—don't rush and don't hurt yourself!
Take it easy and have fun working at your own comfortable pace.

Useful tools:

Craft knife
A craft knife works best when you want to make a clean cut. Choose one that is small and easy for you to hold, and use it until you feel comfortable with it. X-ACTO knives are also very good for making accurate cuts.

Blades for craft knife
Be generous and change the blade often when it gets dull after some use. Dull blades will not only give you unclean edges on the cut paper but they can also cause the knife to slip and cut your finger! When you're done using a blade, be sure to keep it in a small bottle or a container for proper disposal.

Cutting mat
It's important to place this mat under the paper when you cut it with a craft knife. It will keep your table from being damaged and also give a clean cut edge.

Scissors
Scissors come in handy when you want to separate parts before cutting them out more precisely with a craft knife. You may also want to use scissors to cut curves and small parts before you've gotten accustomed to using the knife.

Ruler
Always use a ruler when you cut the model with a craft knife or when you score the folding line. If you haven't gotten used to the craft knife, aluminum or steel rulers are better to use than plastic or wood, because you might accidentally cut into and damage them. Triangular rulers also come in handy.

White PVA-type craft glue
Water-based wood glue or white Elmer's craft glue are well suited for paper crafts. Glue should turn clear when it dries. Glue sticks don't work well for paper crafts.

Stylus with rounded point
By scoring a light groove along the folding line of a paper model, you can make a clean fold. You can get something called a "bone folder" in craft or art supply stores. If you can't find a bone folder, you can use a ballpoint pen that's out of ink or any stylus with a pointed tip, but don't use anything too sharp—it will damage the model part you're folding or even rip right through it. When you score the lines, be sure to do it on a cutting mat or some thick paper.

Compass-type circle cutter
This compasslike instrument with a blade is used to cut out a perfect circle of any radius. Don't try to cut out a circle in just one stroke—cut out the circle with a few short strokes, turning the compass slowly around the fixed center point.

Double-sided tape
When attaching two large surfaces, using craft glue may not be a good idea, because the moisture of the glue will buckle the paper. In such a case, you can instead use double-sided tape. But be careful—once the tape is attached, you can't move its position.

Tweezers
Tweezers are used to build very small parts or inner parts into which your fingers cannot reach. It's a good idea to have two different kinds of tweezers, one with a pointed tip and another with a flat tip.

Toothpicks
Toothpicks are used as "brushes" to apply glue to paper surfaces. They can get clotted with glue after a few uses, so it's a good idea to have a few spares.

Tips as you work:

Cutting

Gently pull off the model page from the spine of the book (A). After roughly separating the parts with scissors, cut them out carefully with a craft knife, using a ruler for straight edges (B). For circular parts it's best to use a circle cutter (C); if you don't have one, try placing the knife in one spot and rotating the paper. If you're cutting out a few different parts at once, use a pencil to write the number on the back to avoid a mix-up.

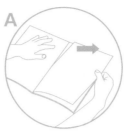

Be careful not to tear the paper. If it doesn't come off the spine, use a craft knife to cut it.

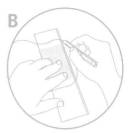

Cover the part you want to cut out with the ruler, to avoid cutting into the part accidentally.

Test the circle cutter on the margin of the page until you feel comfortable using it.

Folding

To make a hill fold, fold so that the front side of the paper is facing out. With a valley fold, the front side should be facing in (A). Use a ruler and a stylus or bone folder to score the folding line (B). Score gently over a few times so as not to damage the paper. All folding lines should be scored and folded before the parts are attached. For the best results, mark the ends of the folding line with a stylus, flip the part, and score the folding line from the back, so that the front surface of the fold remains perfectly clean (C).

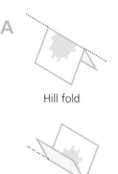

Hill fold

Valley fold

With small parts, it is better to score before you cut them out.

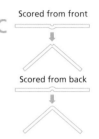

Scored from front

Scored from back

Scored on the backside of the paper, the front surface stays neat and perfect.

Assembling

Before you start gluing the parts, try assembling them without glue, to think about the order in which they should be attached. Parts with curves should be curled first before being glued (A). Don't apply glue directly from the bottle; pour some out on scrap paper and apply evenly using a toothpick (B). After you attach the parts, wait for the glue to dry completely (C). Wash your hands often so they don't get too sticky!

Wrap the part around something like a pen to make it curl.

Don't put glue on too many parts at once—they'll begin to dry before you attach them!

Use tweezers to attach small parts. When making a square rod, you can flatten the part before applying glue.

Coloring

Try making your original karakuri using coloring tools such as markers, watercolor paint, and colored pencils. Do be careful using watercolors—if you paint a large surface, the moisture may cause it to buckle. To color a large surface, it's better to paint a separate paper to cut and attach to the model using double-sided tape or spray glue. If you are used to making paper models, you may paint the model parts before cutting them out, let them dry flat, cut them out, and then start building.

Making it your own

You can customize your paper-craft model by changing the shape of a cam or the length of a rod, or attaching other pieces of your design. You can use tracing paper to trace the parts and transfer them onto thick paper to make your original parts, or you can use the computer to design and print out the parts. There is software for most computers that lets you draw shapes easily, so you may want to try using that if you have a computer at home.

Cam A

The rod makes a repetitious vertical motion.

MODEL ▶ p.65–67   *Please also use parts on p.105 when making a connected model.
EXPLANATION ▶ p.22

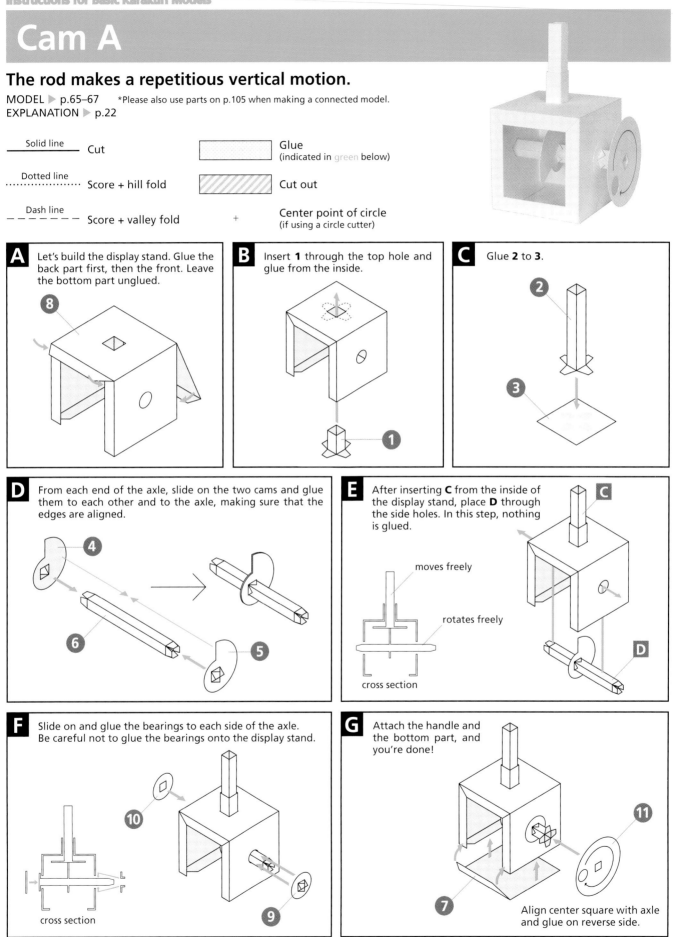

_____ Solid line — Cut

············· Dotted line — Score + hill fold

— — — — — Dash line — Score + valley fold

Glue
(indicated in green below)

Cut out

+ Center point of circle
(if using a circle cutter)

A Let's build the display stand. Glue the back part first, then the front. Leave the bottom part unglued.

8

B Insert **1** through the top hole and glue from the inside.

1

C Glue **2** to **3**.

2

3

D From each end of the axle, slide on the two cams and glue them to each other and to the axle, making sure that the edges are aligned.

4

6

5

E After inserting **C** from the inside of the display stand, place **D** through the side holes. In this step, nothing is glued.

C

moves freely

rotates freely

cross section

D

F Slide on and glue the bearings to each side of the axle. Be careful not to glue the bearings onto the display stand.

10

9

cross section

G Attach the handle and the bottom part, and you're done!

11

7

Align center square with axle and glue on reverse side.

Cam B

Two rods make a vertical movement alternately.

MODEL ▶ p.69–71   *Please also use parts on p.105 when making a connected model.
EXPLANATION ▶ p.22

—— Solid line Cut	▭ Glue (indicated in green below)
····· Dotted line Score + hill fold	▨ Cut out
— — — Dash line Score + valley fold	+ Center point of a circle (if using a circle cutter)

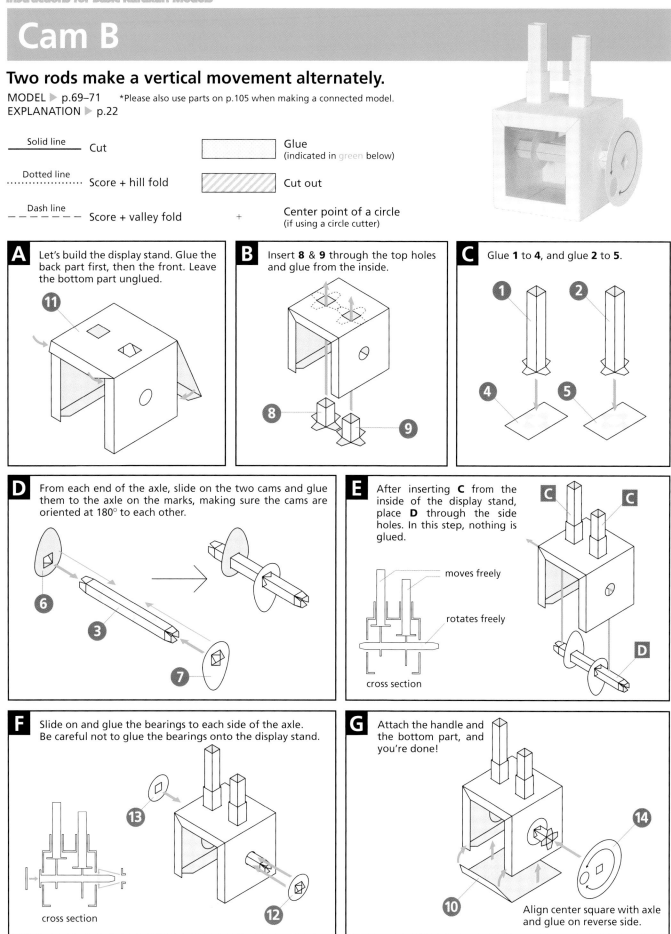

A Let's build the display stand. Glue the back part first, then the front. Leave the bottom part unglued.

B Insert **8** & **9** through the top holes and glue from the inside.

C Glue **1** to **4**, and glue **2** to **5**.

D From each end of the axle, slide on the two cams and glue them to the axle on the marks, making sure the cams are oriented at 180° to each other.

E After inserting **C** from the inside of the display stand, place **D** through the side holes. In this step, nothing is glued.

moves freely
rotates freely
cross section

F Slide on and glue the bearings to each side of the axle. Be careful not to glue the bearings onto the display stand.

cross section

G Attach the handle and the bottom part, and you're done!

Align center square with axle and glue on reverse side.

Cam C

The rod makes a repetitious horizontal movement.

MODEL ▶ p.73–75   *Please also use parts on p.105 when making a connected model.
EXPLANATION ▶ p.22

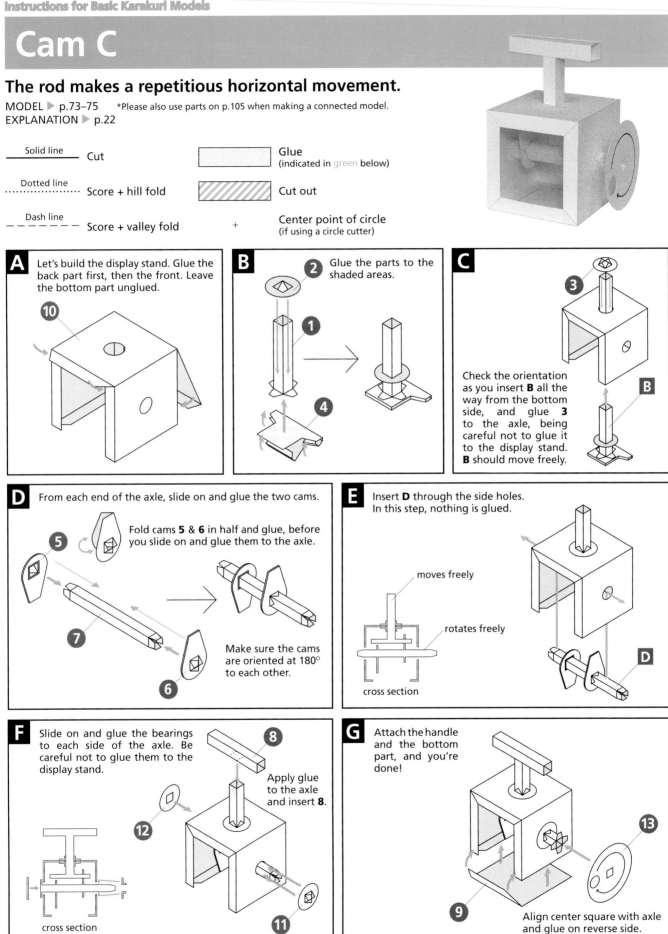

Solid line ——— Cut

Dotted line ·············· Score + hill fold

Dash line — — — — — Score + valley fold

Glue (indicated in green below)

Cut out

+ Center point of circle (if using a circle cutter)

A Let's build the display stand. Glue the back part first, then the front. Leave the bottom part unglued.

B Glue the parts to the shaded areas.

C Check the orientation as you insert **B** all the way from the bottom side, and glue **3** to the axle, being careful not to glue it to the display stand. **B** should move freely.

D From each end of the axle, slide on and glue the two cams.

Fold cams **5** & **6** in half and glue, before you slide on and glue them to the axle.

Make sure the cams are oriented at 180° to each other.

E Insert **D** through the side holes. In this step, nothing is glued.

moves freely

rotates freely

cross section

F Slide on and glue the bearings to each side of the axle. Be careful not to glue them to the display stand.

Apply glue to the axle and insert **8**.

cross section

G Attach the handle and the bottom part, and you're done!

Align center square with axle and glue on reverse side.

Cam D

The rod slides repeatedly in a linear motion.

MODEL ▶ p.77–79   *Please also use parts on p.105 when making a connected model.
EXPLANATION ▶ p.22

———— Solid line   Cut

···················· Dotted line   Score + hill fold

— — — — — Dash line   Score + valley fold

Glue
(indicated in green below)

Cut out

+   Center point of a circle
(if using a circle cutter)

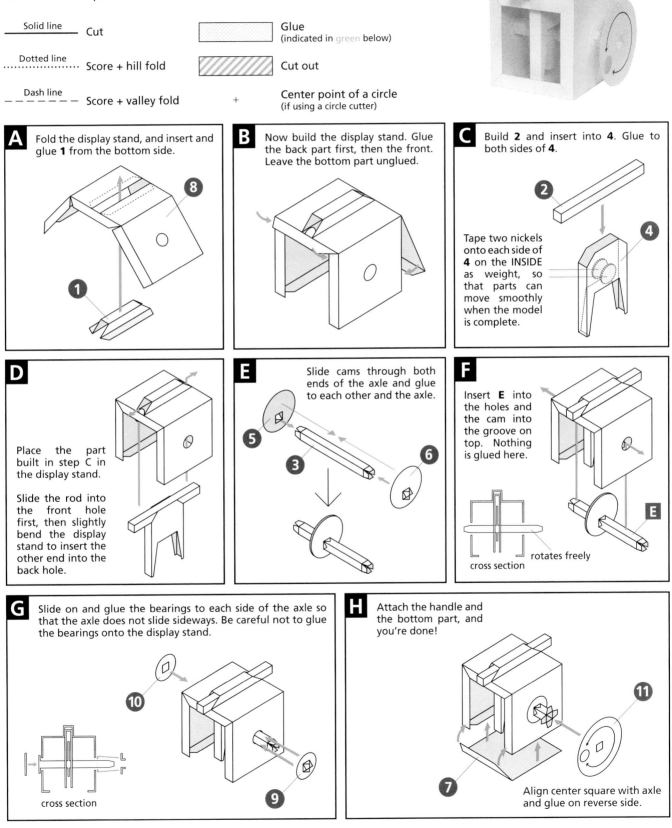

A Fold the display stand, and insert and glue **1** from the bottom side.

B Now build the display stand. Glue the back part first, then the front. Leave the bottom part unglued.

C Build **2** and insert into **4**. Glue to both sides of **4**.

Tape two nickels onto each side of **4** on the INSIDE as weight, so that parts can move smoothly when the model is complete.

D Place the part built in step C in the display stand.

Slide the rod into the front hole first, then slightly bend the display stand to insert the other end into the back hole.

E Slide cams through both ends of the axle and glue to each other and the axle.

F Insert **E** into the holes and the cam into the groove on top. Nothing is glued here.

rotates freely
cross section

G Slide on and glue the bearings to each side of the axle so that the axle does not slide sideways. Be careful not to glue the bearings onto the display stand.

cross section

H Attach the handle and the bottom part, and you're done!

Align center square with axle and glue on reverse side.

Crank C (Slider-crank)

The turning of a crank is converted into a vertical motion.

MODEL ▶ p.89–91
EXPLANATION ▶ p.24

——————— Solid line **Cut**	▦ **Glue** (indicated in green below)
···················· Dotted line **Score + hill fold**	▨ **Cut out**
– – – – – – Dash line **Score + valley fold**	+ **Center point of circle** (if using a circle cutter)

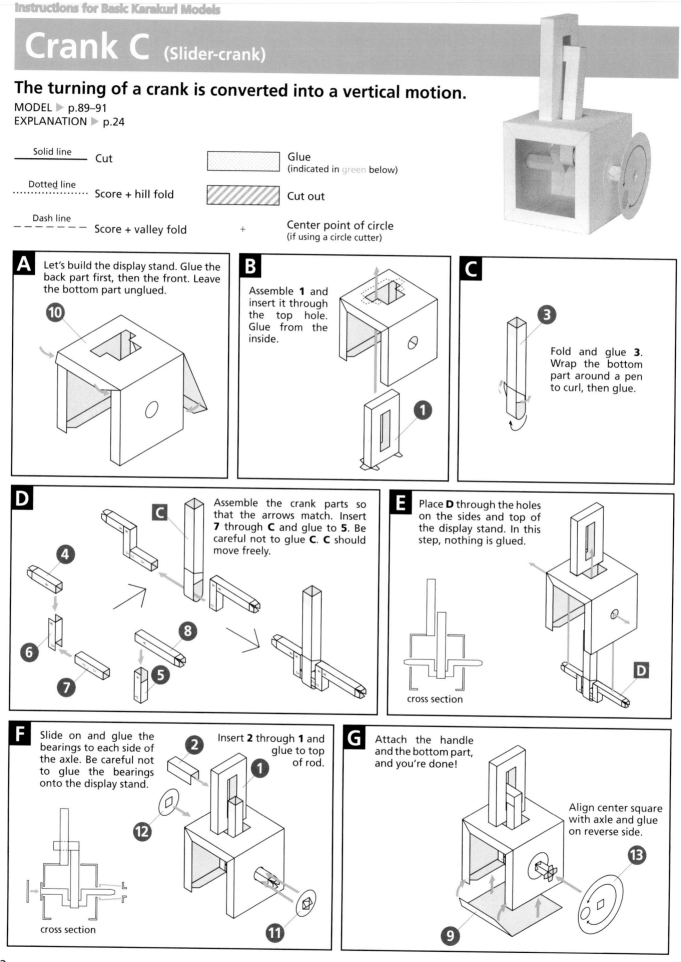

A Let's build the display stand. Glue the back part first, then the front. Leave the bottom part unglued.

10

B Assemble **1** and insert it through the top hole. Glue from the inside.

1

C Fold and glue **3**. Wrap the bottom part around a pen to curl, then glue.

3

D Assemble the crank parts so that the arrows match. Insert **7** through **C** and glue to **5**. Be careful not to glue **C**. **C** should move freely.

4 **C** **6** **7** **8** **5**

E Place **D** through the holes on the sides and top of the display stand. In this step, nothing is glued.

cross section

D

F Slide on and glue the bearings to each side of the axle. Be careful not to glue the bearings onto the display stand.

Insert **2** through **1** and glue to top of rod.

2 **1** **12** **11**

cross section

G Attach the handle and the bottom part, and you're done!

Align center square with axle and glue on reverse side.

13 **9**

42

Gear A

The gear turns horizontally to the handle.

MODEL ▶ p.93–95   *Please also use parts on p.105 when making a connected model.
EXPLANATION ▶ p.26

—————— Solid line **Cut**	▦ **Glue** (indicated in green below)
·················· Dotted line **Score + hill fold**	▨ **Cut out**
– – – – – Dash line **Score + valley fold**	+ **Center point of a circle** (if using a circle cutter)

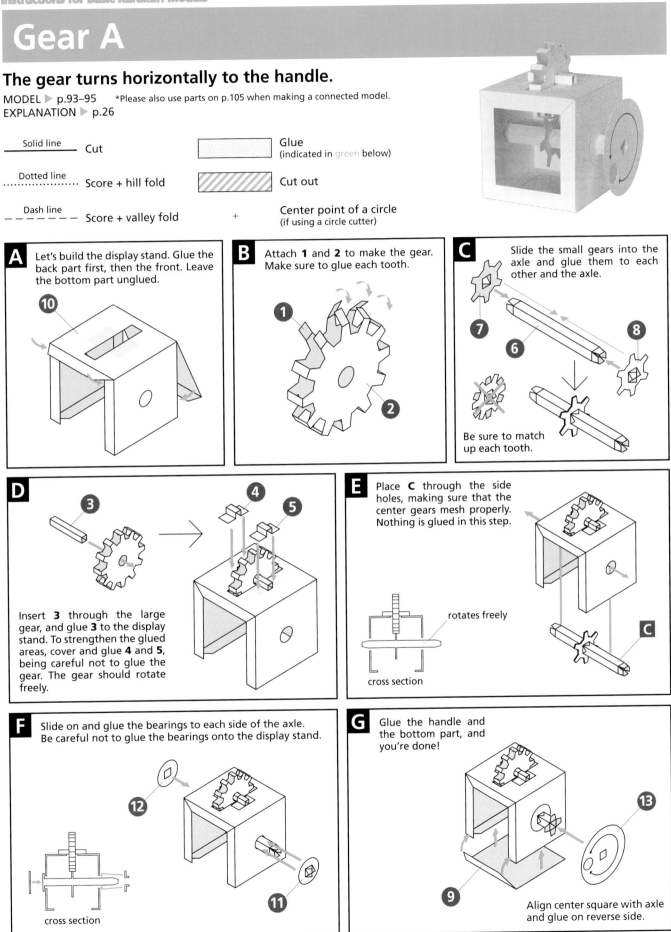

A Let's build the display stand. Glue the back part first, then the front. Leave the bottom part unglued.

B Attach **1** and **2** to make the gear. Make sure to glue each tooth.

C Slide the small gears into the axle and glue them to each other and the axle.

Be sure to match up each tooth.

D Insert **3** through the large gear, and glue **3** to the display stand. To strengthen the glued areas, cover and glue **4** and **5**, being careful not to glue the gear. The gear should rotate freely.

E Place **C** through the side holes, making sure that the center gears mesh properly. Nothing is glued in this step.

rotates freely

cross section

F Slide on and glue the bearings to each side of the axle. Be careful not to glue the bearings onto the display stand.

cross section

G Glue the handle and the bottom part, and you're done!

Align center square with axle and glue on reverse side.

43

Gear B

The gear turns perpendicularly to the handle.

MODEL ▶ p.97–99   *Please also use parts on p.105 when making a connected model.
EXPLANATION ▶ p.26

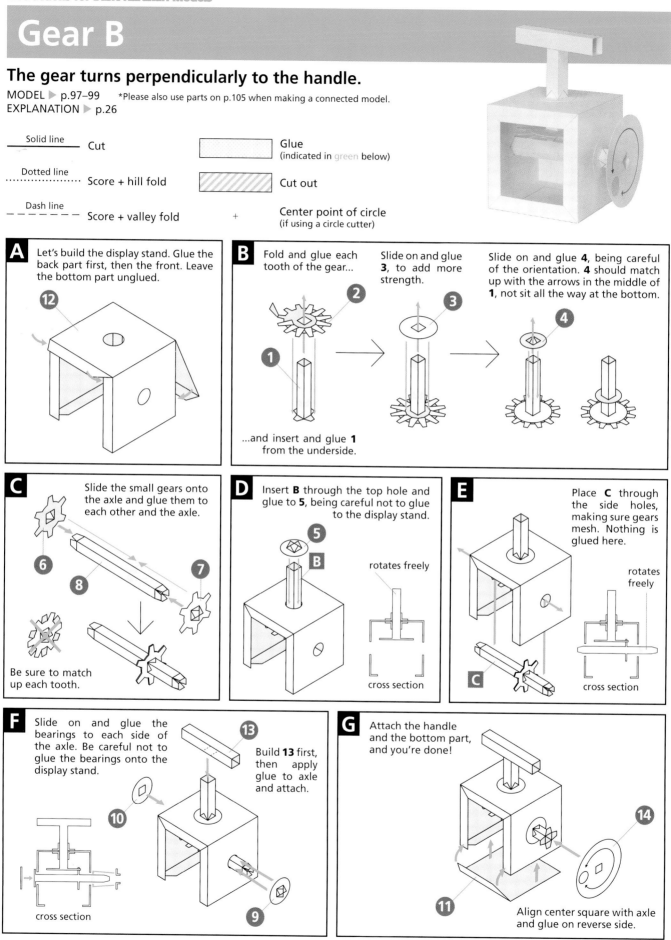

Solid line ——— Cut

Dotted line ·········· Score + hill fold

Dash line – – – – – Score + valley fold

▨ Glue (indicated in green below)

▨ Cut out

+ Center point of circle (if using a circle cutter)

A Let's build the display stand. Glue the back part first, then the front. Leave the bottom part unglued.

12

B Fold and glue each tooth of the gear...

...and insert and glue **1** from the underside.

Slide on and glue **3**, to add more strength.

Slide on and glue **4**, being careful of the orientation. **4** should match up with the arrows in the middle of **1**, not sit all the way at the bottom.

C Slide the small gears onto the axle and glue them to each other and the axle.

Be sure to match up each tooth.

D Insert **B** through the top hole and glue to **5**, being careful not to glue to the display stand.

rotates freely

cross section

E Place **C** through the side holes, making sure gears mesh. Nothing is glued here.

rotates freely

cross section

F Slide on and glue the bearings to each side of the axle. Be careful not to glue the bearings onto the display stand.

Build **13** first, then apply glue to axle and attach.

cross section

G Attach the handle and the bottom part, and you're done!

Align center square with axle and glue on reverse side.

Geneva Stop

The wheel turns in a discontinuous rhythm.

MODEL ▶ p101–103   *Please also use parts on p.105 when making a connected model.
EXPLANATION ▶ p.30

——— Solid line Cut	░░░ Glue (indicated in green below)
·········· Dotted line Score + hill fold	▨ Cut out
— — — Dash line Score + valley fold	+ Center point of a circle (if using a circle cutter)

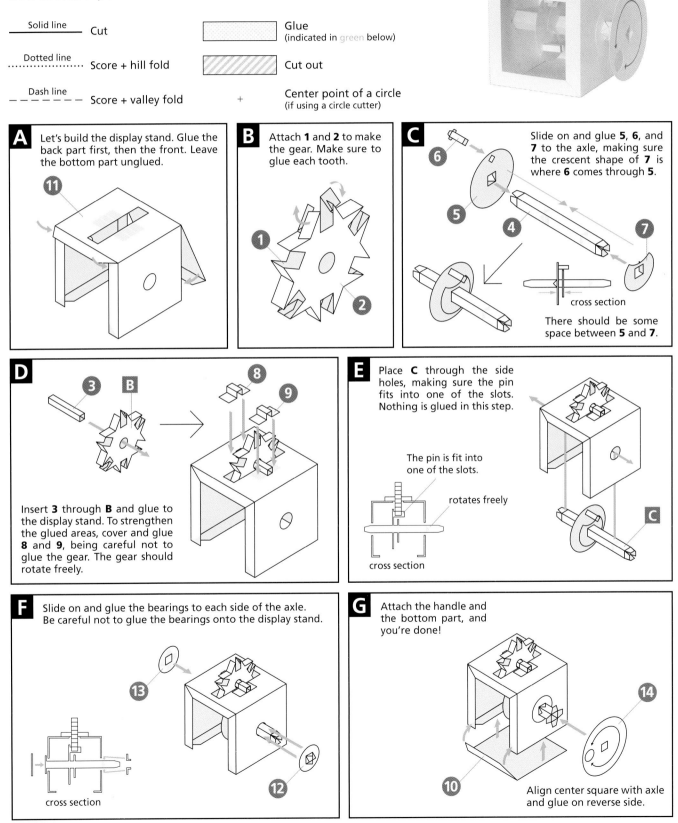

A Let's build the display stand. Glue the back part first, then the front. Leave the bottom part unglued.

11

B Attach **1** and **2** to make the gear. Make sure to glue each tooth.

1
2

C Slide on and glue **5**, **6**, and **7** to the axle, making sure the crescent shape of **7** is where **6** comes through **5**.

6
5
4
7

cross section

There should be some space between **5** and **7**.

D
3 B
8
9

Insert **3** through **B** and glue to the display stand. To strengthen the glued areas, cover and glue **8** and **9**, being careful not to glue the gear. The gear should rotate freely.

E Place **C** through the side holes, making sure the pin fits into one of the slots. Nothing is glued in this step.

The pin is fit into one of the slots.

rotates freely

C

cross section

F Slide on and glue the bearings to each side of the axle. Be careful not to glue the bearings onto the display stand.

13
12

cross section

G Attach the handle and the bottom part, and you're done!

14
10

Align center square with axle and glue on reverse side.

45

Tea-Serving Robot

The robot's head bobs up and down as he moves forward.
Will he deliver the teacup without knocking it over?

MODEL ▶ p.113–115

Solid line — Cut	Glue (indicated in green below)
Dotted line ⋯⋯⋯ Score + hill fold	Cut out
Dash line — — — Score + valley fold	+ Center point of circle (if using a circle cutter)

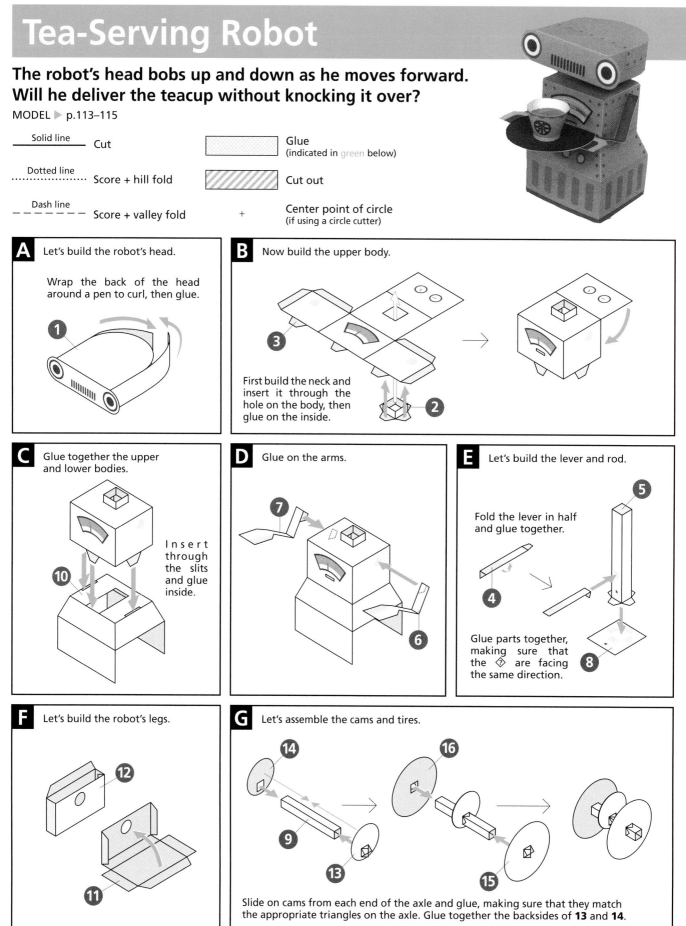

A Let's build the robot's head.

Wrap the back of the head around a pen to curl, then glue.

B Now build the upper body.

First build the neck and insert it through the hole on the body, then glue on the inside.

C Glue together the upper and lower bodies.

Insert through the slits and glue inside.

D Glue on the arms.

E Let's build the lever and rod.

Fold the lever in half and glue together.

Glue parts together, making sure that the ◇ are facing the same direction.

F Let's build the robot's legs.

G Let's assemble the cams and tires.

Slide on cams from each end of the axle and glue, making sure that they match the appropriate triangles on the axle. Glue together the backsides of **13** and **14**.

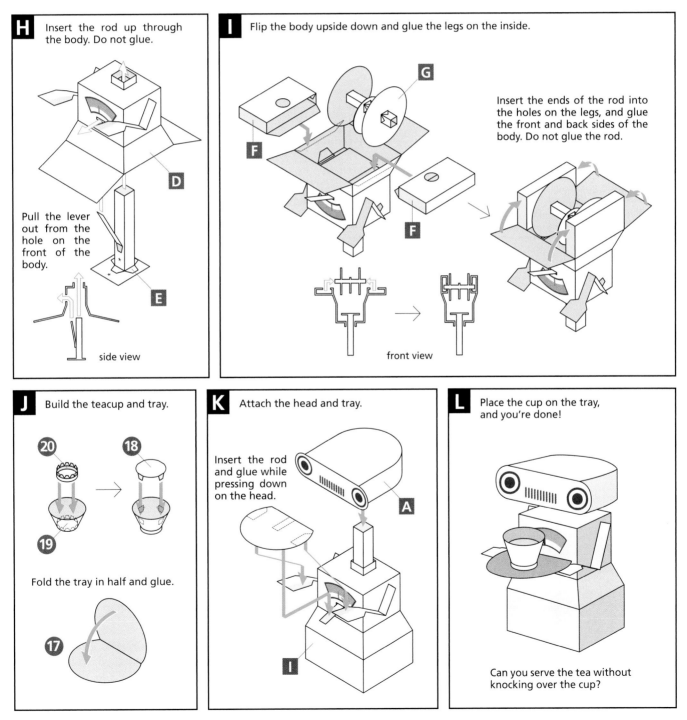

H Insert the rod up through the body. Do not glue.

D

E

Pull the lever out from the hole on the front of the body.

side view

I Flip the body upside down and glue the legs on the inside.

G

F

F

Insert the ends of the rod into the holes on the legs, and glue the front and back sides of the body. Do not glue the rod.

front view

J Build the teacup and tray.

20   18

19

Fold the tray in half and glue.

17

K Attach the head and tray.

Insert the rod and glue while pressing down on the head.

A

I

L Place the cup on the tray, and you're done!

Can you serve the tea without knocking over the cup?

Ready to Fly

The persistent penguin keeps flapping his wings, hoping to fly. Who knows, maybe one day he really will take off!

MODEL ▶ p.117–123

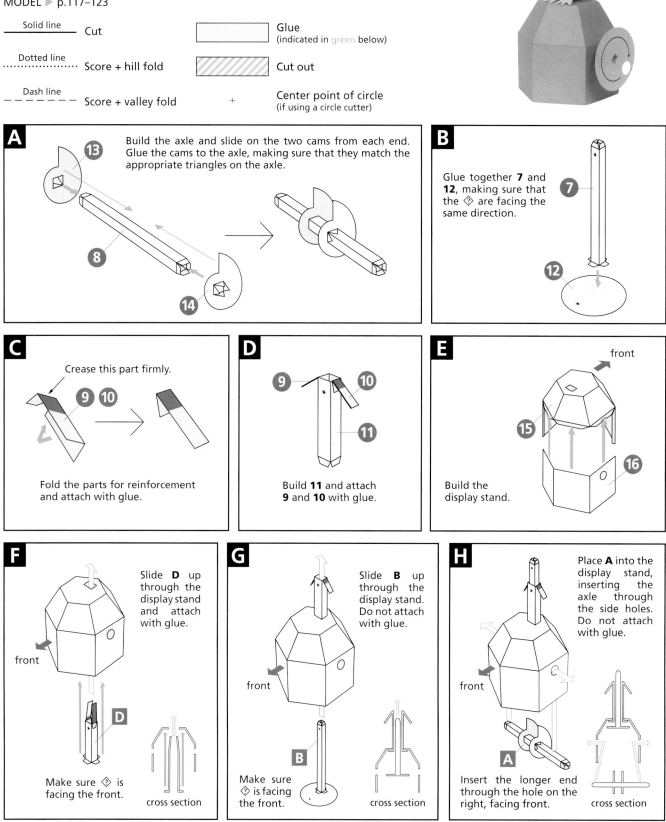

——————— Solid line	Cut
·················· Dotted line	Score + hill fold
— — — — — Dash line	Score + valley fold

Glue
(indicated in green below)

Cut out

+ Center point of circle
(if using a circle cutter)

A Build the axle and slide on the two cams from each end. Glue the cams to the axle, making sure that they match the appropriate triangles on the axle.

B Glue together **7** and **12**, making sure that the ◇ are facing the same direction.

C Crease this part firmly.

Fold the parts for reinforcement and attach with glue.

D Build **11** and attach **9** and **10** with glue.

E Build the display stand.

front

F Slide **D** up through the display stand and attach with glue.

front

Make sure ◇ is facing the front.

cross section

G Slide **B** up through the display stand. Do not attach with glue.

front

Make sure ◇ is facing the front.

cross section

H Place **A** into the display stand, inserting the axle through the side holes. Do not attach with glue.

front

Insert the longer end through the hole on the right, facing front.

cross section

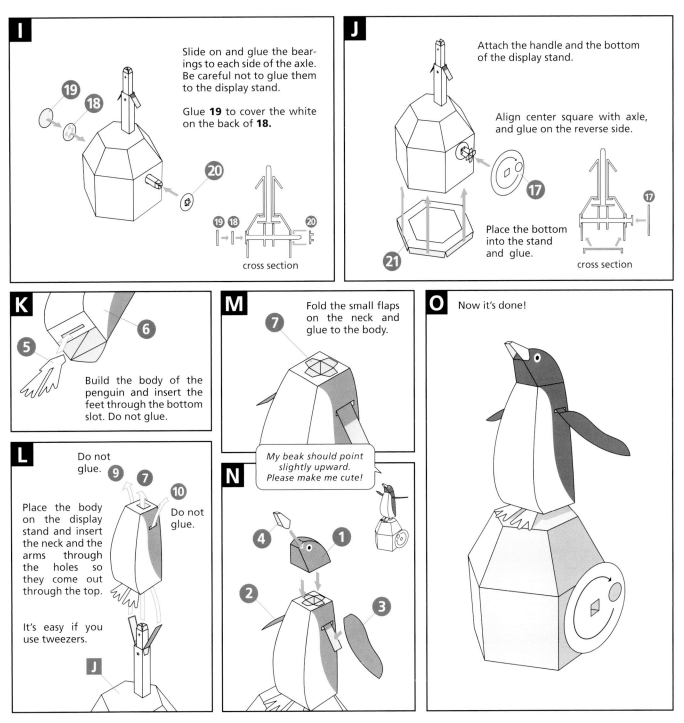

I

Slide on and glue the bearings to each side of the axle. Be careful not to glue them to the display stand.

Glue **19** to cover the white on the back of **18.**

cross section

J

Attach the handle and the bottom of the display stand.

Align center square with axle, and glue on the reverse side.

Place the bottom into the stand and glue.

cross section

K

Build the body of the penguin and insert the feet through the bottom slot. Do not glue.

L

Do not glue.

Do not glue.

Place the body on the display stand and insert the neck and the arms through the holes so they come out through the top.

It's easy if you use tweezers.

M

Fold the small flaps on the neck and glue to the body.

My beak should point slightly upward. Please make me cute!

N

O

Now it's done!

Peek-a-Bear

A cute bear wants to play peekaboo with you!
Have fun pacing the speed as you turn the handle.

MODEL ▶ p.125–131

—————— Solid line **Cut**	▦ **Glue** (indicated in green below)
·············· Dotted line **Score + hill fold**	▨ **Cut out**
— — — — Dash line **Score + valley fold**	+ **Center point of circle** (if using a circle cutter)

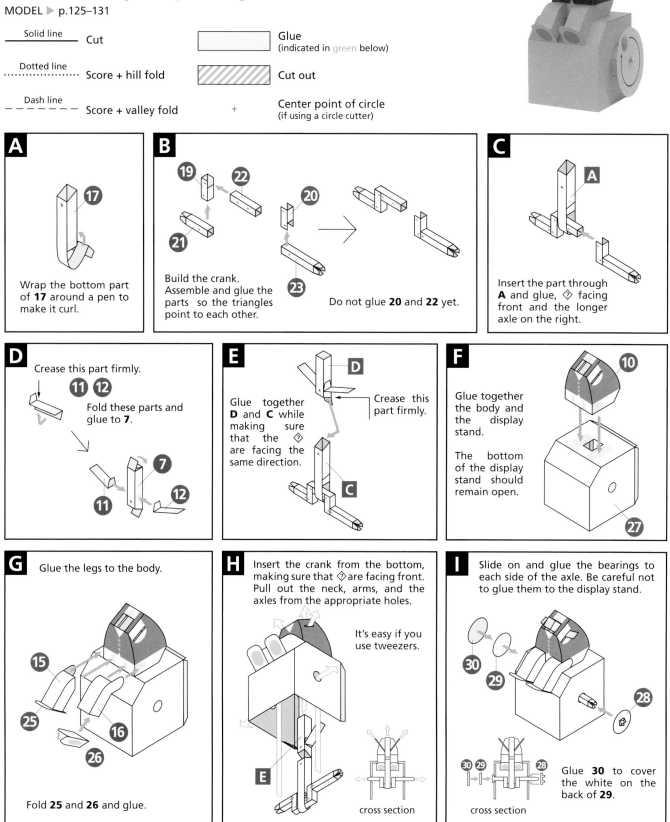

A
Wrap the bottom part of **17** around a pen to make it curl.

B
Build the crank. Assemble and glue the parts so the triangles point to each other.
Do not glue **20** and **22** yet.

C
Insert the part through **A** and glue, ◇ facing front and the longer axle on the right.

D
Crease this part firmly.
Fold these parts and glue to **7**.

E
Glue together **D** and **C** while making sure that the ◇ are facing the same direction.
Crease this part firmly.

F
Glue together the body and the display stand.
The bottom of the display stand should remain open.

G
Glue the legs to the body.
Fold **25** and **26** and glue.

H
Insert the crank from the bottom, making sure that ◇ are facing front. Pull out the neck, arms, and the axles from the appropriate holes.
It's easy if you use tweezers.
cross section

I
Slide on and glue the bearings to each side of the axle. Be careful not to glue them to the display stand.
Glue **30** to cover the white on the back of **29**.
cross section

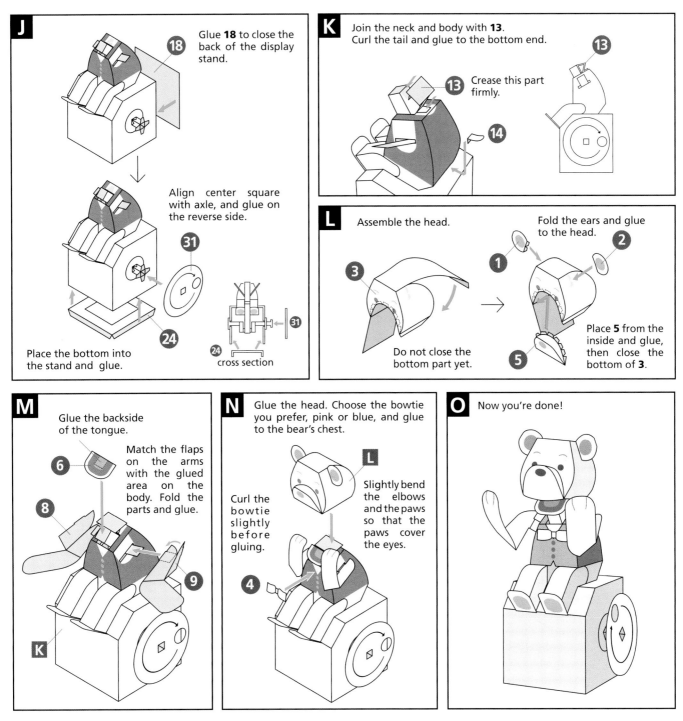

J Glue **18** to close the back of the display stand.

Align center square with axle, and glue on the reverse side.

Place the bottom into the stand and glue.

cross section

K Join the neck and body with **13**.
Curl the tail and glue to the bottom end.

Crease this part firmly.

L Assemble the head.

Fold the ears and glue to the head.

Do not close the bottom part yet.

Place **5** from the inside and glue, then close the bottom of **3**.

M Glue the backside of the tongue.

Match the flaps on the arms with the glued area on the body. Fold the parts and glue.

N Glue the head. Choose the bowtie you prefer, pink or blue, and glue to the bear's chest.

Curl the bowtie slightly before gluing.

Slightly bend the elbows and the paws so that the paws cover the eyes.

O Now you're done!

Wild Wild West

A steam engine dashes through the wild desert of the West. Watch as it runs in and out of the rocky mountain tunnel!

MODEL ▶ p.113–143

Solid line — Cut	Glue (indicated in green below)
Dotted line ⋯⋯ Score + hill fold	Cut out
Dash line − − − Score + valley fold	+ Center point of circle (if using a circle cutter)

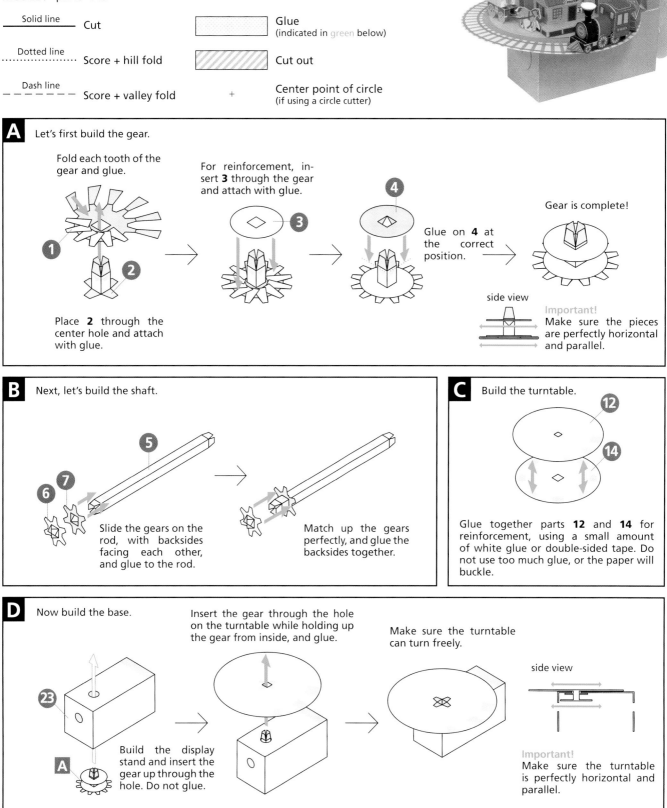

A Let's first build the gear.

Fold each tooth of the gear and glue.

For reinforcement, insert **3** through the gear and attach with glue.

Glue on **4** at the correct position.

Gear is complete!

Place **2** through the center hole and attach with glue.

side view

Important! Make sure the pieces are perfectly horizontal and parallel.

B Next, let's build the shaft.

Slide the gears on the rod, with backsides facing each other, and glue to the rod.

Match up the gears perfectly, and glue the backsides together.

C Build the turntable.

Glue together parts **12** and **14** for reinforcement, using a small amount of white glue or double-sided tape. Do not use too much glue, or the paper will buckle.

D Now build the base.

Insert the gear through the hole on the turntable while holding up the gear from inside, and glue.

Make sure the turntable can turn freely.

side view

Build the display stand and insert the gear up through the hole. Do not glue.

Important! Make sure the turntable is perfectly horizontal and parallel.

52

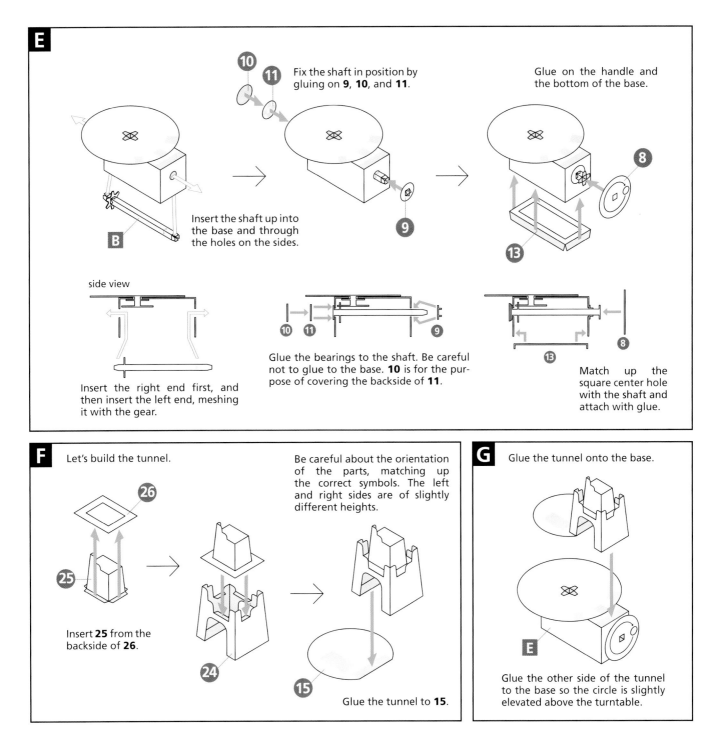

E

Fix the shaft in position by gluing on **9**, **10**, and **11**.

Glue on the handle and the bottom of the base.

Insert the shaft up into the base and through the holes on the sides.

side view

Insert the right end first, and then insert the left end, meshing it with the gear.

Glue the bearings to the shaft. Be careful not to glue to the base. **10** is for the purpose of covering the backside of **11**.

Match up the square center hole with the shaft and attach with glue.

F

Let's build the tunnel.

Be careful about the orientation of the parts, matching up the correct symbols. The left and right sides are of slightly different heights.

Insert **25** from the backside of **26**.

Glue the tunnel to **15**.

G

Glue the tunnel onto the base.

Glue the other side of the tunnel to the base so the circle is slightly elevated above the turntable.

Wild Wild West (continued)

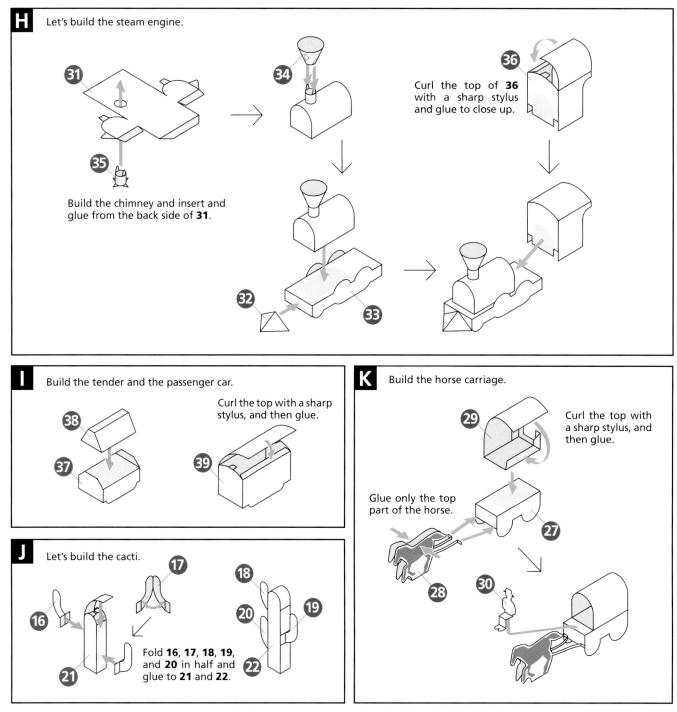

H Let's build the steam engine.

Curl the top of **36** with a sharp stylus and glue to close up.

Build the chimney and insert and glue from the back side of **31**.

I Build the tender and the passenger car.

Curl the top with a sharp stylus, and then glue.

K Build the horse carriage.

Curl the top with a sharp stylus, and then glue.

Glue only the top part of the horse.

J Let's build the cacti.

Fold **16**, **17**, **18**, **19**, and **20** in half and glue to **21** and **22**.

L Let's build the station.

M Glue the steam engine, tender and passenger car onto the outer edge of the turntable on the railroad tracks.

N Glue the station, cacti, and horse carriage onto the inner circle **15**.

Place the cacti and the horse carriage wherever you see fit.

O And you're finished!

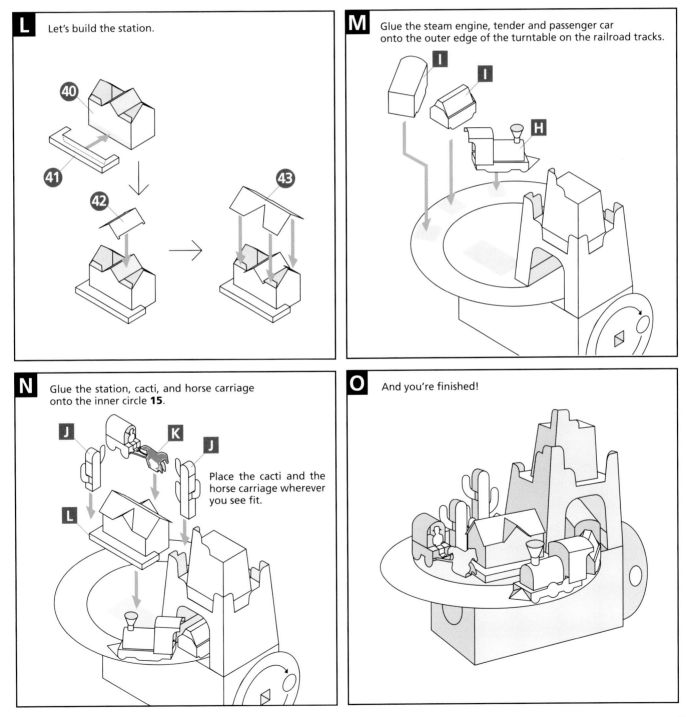

"Let's do this one!" "No, that looks hard!" "How about this one?" My students were excitedly discussing the karakuri models.

Let me tell you a little bit about myself. I am a high school physics teacher. Paper craft is an important teaching tool for me. I develop paper crafts of my own and use them to teach the students in my classes. As I place the paper models in front of me and study them from various angles, I begin to see that various laws of physics that at first seem to have totally different qualities—such as size, shape, color, and texture—actually exist in unison. The world of art and the world of physics: I feel that there's always a connection.

In the professional study of physics, we use very complicated equations in order to express or calculate various natural phenomena. In high school physics, however, there are visual aids such as charts and graphs that help students use their imagination and understand better. I think this is one of the greatest things about high school physics.

Every spring when the new school year starts, I begin teaching students who have no knowledge of physics—they're "green," so to speak. But then we soon enter a long summer vacation. So I was looking for a good summer project for the students to do at home that would keep what they learned during the spring semester fresh in their minds, gear their interest toward physics, stimulate their curiosity, and prepare their minds for an exciting semester in the fall.

It was in March 2006 that I first met Keisuke Saka. He showed me the manuscript of his book *Karakuri*. Stick a finger inside a little hole and turn the handle clockwise, and a weird-shaped square axle rotates and moves a crank. That was all there is to it. The paper is smooth and easy to turn, and the square axle directly transmitted the force from the finger. I felt more possibility in this.

How will these models connect? What would my students make of these? I had never used a paper craft that moves in my classes. I became quite excited, and Saka and I agreed to use these kits as my students' summer projects.

So the long-awaited karakuri kits arrived in early July. Of the ten types of karakuri, each student chose just one. I displayed all the models and instructions to take a survey of which ones they wanted to make. The most popular were the gear and cam models, because they seemed pretty simple to make. The second preference varied, so I was able to give each student the kit that he or she preferred.

What would my students come up with? Would it feel more like an art project? I tried making one. I thought I had great ideas, but the models were so beautiful I didn't feel like adding much more to them. And the crank, gear, and cam mechanisms were extremely realistic. I thought, "This might turn out to be a tough project to do over a vacation!" I spent my summer praying that my students were taking on this project well.

September 1 was the first day of class. I had all my students bring their karakuri kits to report on what they had made. I was astounded. What they had come up with went far beyond

More than 100 karakuri paper toys were displayed on the first day of class. It was like a toy museum!

my expectations. High schoolers rock! Each student had documented their process and what they had done to make the models better. One student said, "With my Geneva stop, I had a hard time just trying to make it move." When I heard that, I said, "You're a high schooler, and you're talking professional physics! Just that fact makes your project worthwhile." Once they learned to make the basic models, they said it became much easier to develop them into real karakuri.

At the first physics class of the fall semester, I had everyone's masterpiece displayed on a row of desks in the back of the classroom. Then each student went to their work and turned the karakuri as I slowly slid from one end of the row to the other, recording them with a video camera. The students were to look into the camera, say the title of the work, and turn their piece as two TV monitors showed the recorded footage.

"Uh, what was the title of my thing? I guess I'll just call it 'Untitled.'"

"Which way am I supposed to turn this?"

"Where is the camera?"

"Oh, no, my handle doesn't budge!"

The students all seemed a bit nervous in front of the camera, but a lineup of such a variety of creative karakuri was quite impressive. Students raised their voices in surprise when someone's karakuri made unexpected movements. When we were all done, everyone was smiling. The karakuri show-and-tell turned out to be a lot of fun.

After the show-and-tell session, I displayed the students' works in the physics room for other people to see. Placed all in one row, it was like a paper-craft toy museum! When students from other classes or schools came and saw the works, everyone was quite interested, and, although no one was allowed to touch the works, I think people would have enjoyed trying out the karakuri for themselves and seeing how the parts actually move.

Robots, arguably the pinnacle of scientific technology today, are made of a combination of various karakuri–like mechanisms. There isn't a course on mechanical engineering in high school physics, but karakuri paper craft is a perfect tool to teach students about the lever mechanism, force momentum, and force transmission or conversion. Paper craft is also ideal because it has room for creativity, allowing the students to make their own designs.

And so *Karakuri* has become one of my favorite teaching tools. I hope to further widen the horizon of using paper crafts to get the students excited about learning high school physics.

Masayuki Kobayashi
High School Teacher of Physics
Tama University Hijirigaoka High School, Tokyo, Japan

Author's Biography

Keisuke Saka
Paper engineer/graphic designer
www.zuko.to/kobo/

Born in 1965, Saka graduated from Kobe University, Kobe, Japan, with a degree in literature. After studying visual design at Kuwasawa Design School, in 1994 Saka became a freelance graphic designer and started creating paper-crafts. While living in Denmark from 1997-2000, he was fascinated by European automata, or mechanized puppets. Upon returning to Japan in 2000 he established Zukoshitu, his own paper-engineering/design office. His works include paper-craft kits, advertisements, Web design, magazine contents, and books. He has held paper-craft workshops in various cities in Japan, and in 2008, a series of his workshops were broadcasted on NHK (Japan Broadcasting Corporation), the national TV education program. His "Karakuri Paper-Craft" series is also sold in the U.S. and Europe, available through Noted, Co. (http://www.notedco.com)

Contributors' Biographies

Masayuki Kobayashi
High School Teacher of Physics
Tama University Hijirigaoka High School

(2008–, Teacher of Physics, Tokyo Gakugei University Senior High School)

Born in 1962, Kobayashi graduated from Tokyo Gakugei University with a degree in education. While teaching at Tokyo Metropolitan Katakura High School he involved himself in developing courses in sculpture, after which he began integrating artistic concepts into physics education. He has taught at Tokyo Metropolitan Aoyama High School, in NHK's high school seminar of physics, and at Tama University Hijirigaoka High School. Currently teaching at Tokyo Gakugei University Senior High School, Kobayashi is active in developing physics education using everyday objects and writes high school textbooks and other books on science.

Yasuyuki Shirai
President, Japan Mechanism Art/
Professor, Chiba Institute of Technology

Born in 1941, Shirai graduated from Chiba Institute of Technology with a degree in electrical engineering. After working at Tokyo Institute of Technology Teacher Training Center and advanced mechanical and electrical engineering programs at Chiba Institute of Technology, he is currently head of educational department at Chiba Institute of Technology. Shirai is the founder of Japan Mechanism Art, a study organization of mechanical creativity holding karakuri exhibitions and performances throughout Japan.

Toshio Arai
CEO, Concept Plus Co., Ltd.
www.conceptplus.jp

Born in 1952, Arai graduated from Sophia University with a degree in mechanical engineering in 1976 and began working for Sony Corporation as a technical engineer. He is an important figure in the development of Walkmans, CD Walkmans, and stereos. In 2003, after 27 years at Sony, he established Concept Plus Co., Ltd. His company initiated "Kyouiku Shokunin Project" in 2007 and creates products for people of all ages, with concepts such as "For the children to have a dream in science," and "Protecting our precious Earth."

Translator/Designer's Biography

Eri Hamaji
Translator/graphic designer

Born in 1982, Hamaji graduated from the Cooper Union School of Art, New York, in 2005. After working at Mori Art Museum in Roppongi, Tokyo, she currently translates, coordinates, and designs creative books. She has written and translated for THEME magazine, New York, and translates and designs books for Mark Batty Publisher, LLC., New York, including *Everyman's McLuhan*, *Everyman's Joyce*, *FACE FOOD*, and *Graffiti Japan*.

INDEX

Afterword

In the process of working on paper-craft designs, I give birth to many test models made with simple white paper (in the world of painters they call it a "rough sketch"). I make a lot of test models, especially for karakuri paper-crafts, because a difference of even a few millimeters could affect how the parts move. By the time I finish designing one karakuri, there are countless test models scattered around my desk. I no longer need them because I have the final design done, but they *are* my creations, and I feel bad throwing them away. At one point, I began keeping some of them to display on my shelf. White is the color of a blank canvas, stimulating one's creativity. Just staring at these test models sometimes brings me the best ideas.

One day, when I was turning a handle of one of those test models, waiting for a good idea to come to me, I said to myself, "What if this *is* the final model for a kit? Why not!" Back then, I was making paper-craft kits to sell individually, and I was starting to realize that most tools and machines around us are all made from just a few simple mechanisms, only combined or different in size. I thought, "What if I write a few pages of text to explain those simple mechanisms and make a whole book for beginners?" And that is how this book started.

But of course, it's always easier said than done. I wasn't the best student of physics, and for the first time in my life I dug into a book on mechanical engineering, trying to figure out how to read through these pages full of unfamiliar equations and symbols. If it weren't for Mr. Arai, who patiently stayed with me and my project from beginning to end, Mr. Shirai, who kindly gave me technical advice, and Mr. Kobayashi, who shared with me his great knowledge on how to teach things to other people, it would have been impossible for me to write this book. I also want to thank Mr. Koseki, president (and paper-craft officer) of Shubunsha, the Japanese publisher of the original book, who had to endure my slow progress for a few years after giving me the okay to publish this book, without complaining a bit.

I also want to thank each and every Tama University Hijirigaoka High School student who participated in this project. It gave me the biggest thrill to see everyone's masterpieces displayed in the physics classroom. I will never forget that feeling. I'd like to thank you all very much.

Last but not least, I would like to express my deep gratitude to Ms. BJ Berti who edited this book, Ms. Jasmine Faustino, and everyone at St. Martin's Press. Thank you very much for all your help in publishing this English edition of *Karakuri*. I would also like to thank Ms. Eri Hamaji, who worked on both the translation and the design of this book.

One of the most wonderful things about paper crafts is that you can experience the joy of making something of your own that you can play with and have fun. I was very conscious of leaving a lot of room for your own ideas and creativity in these karakuri paper crafts. My wish is that this book will open a door to your journey to discover the pleasure in making things your own.

Keisuke Saka

Basic Karakuri Models

 These pages are meant to be torn out of the book and cut to be used as building materials for the model.

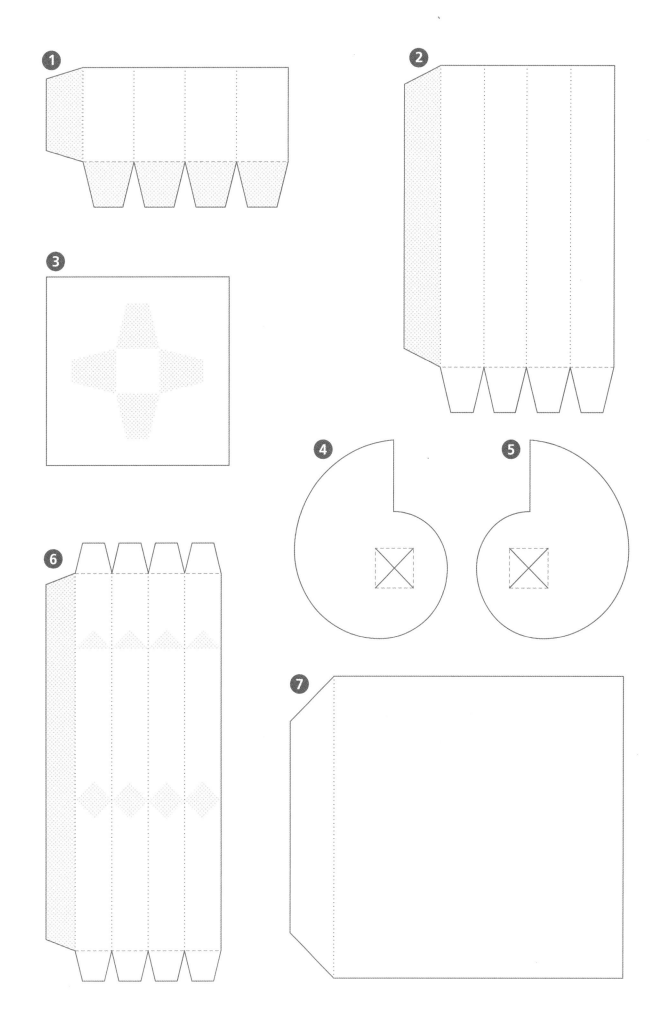

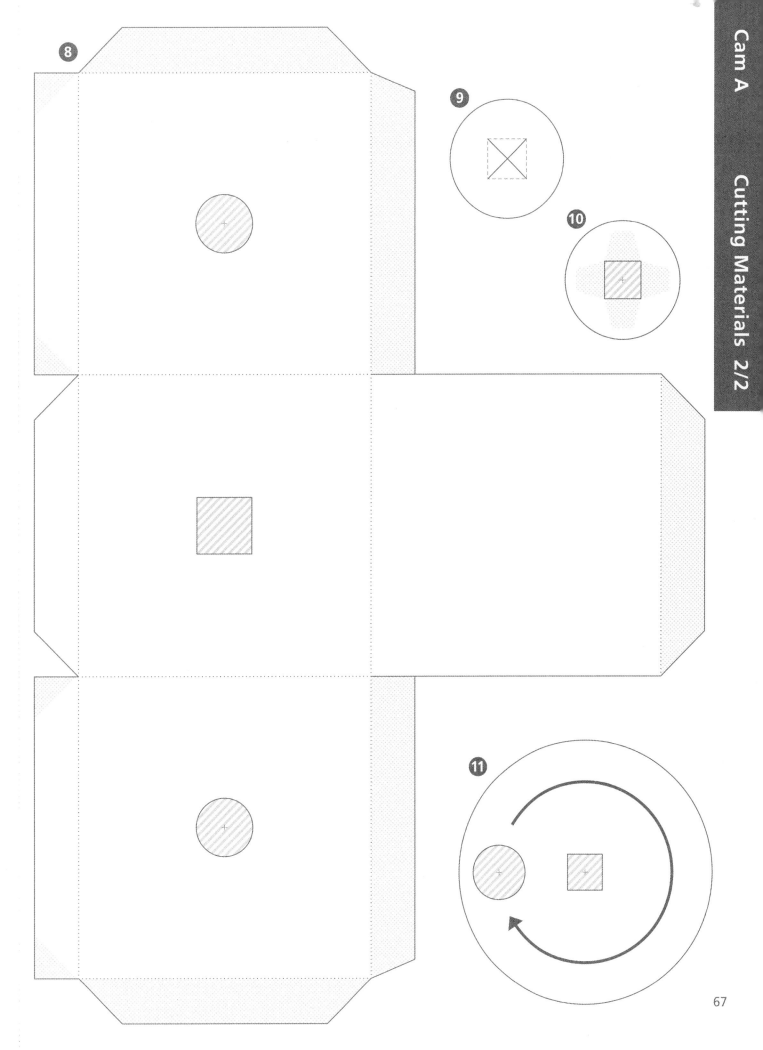

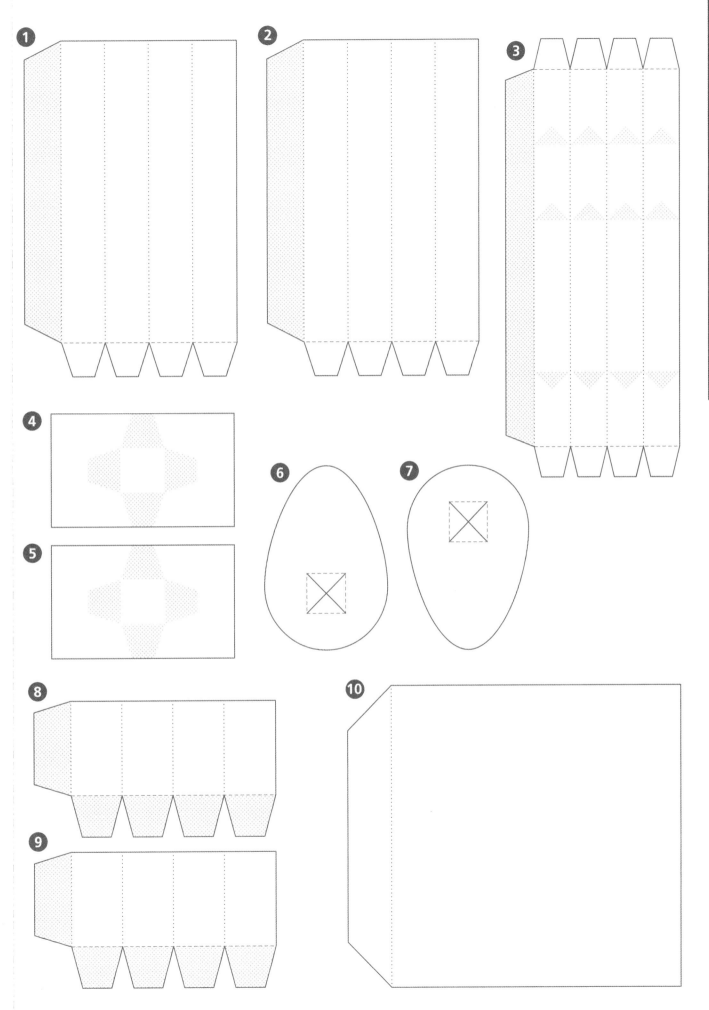

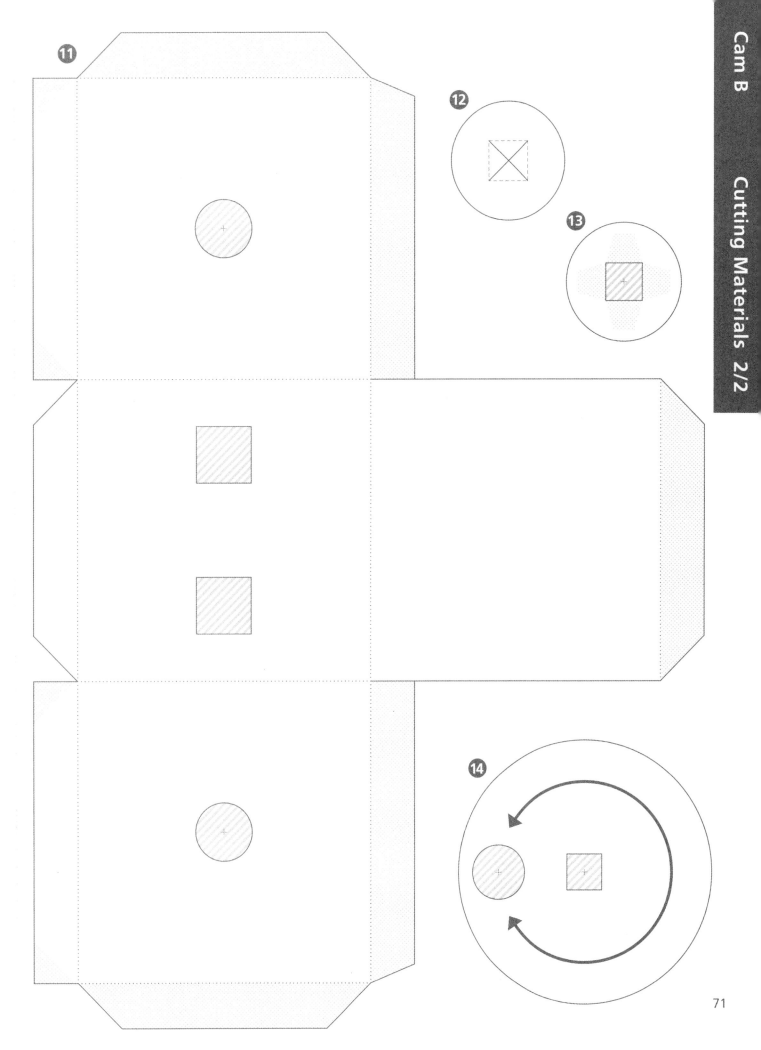

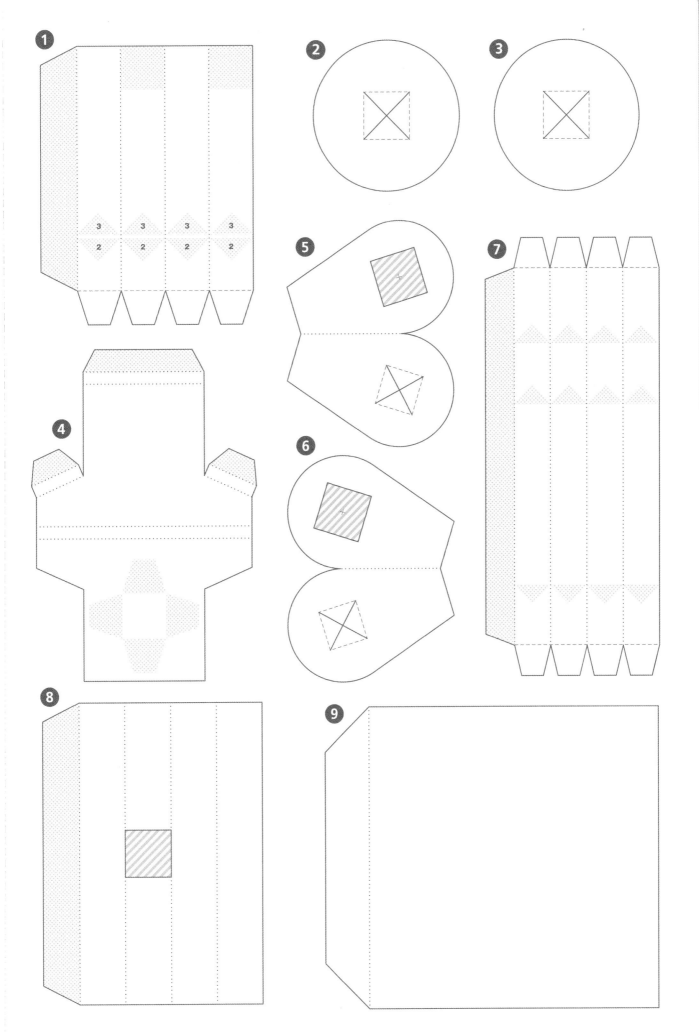

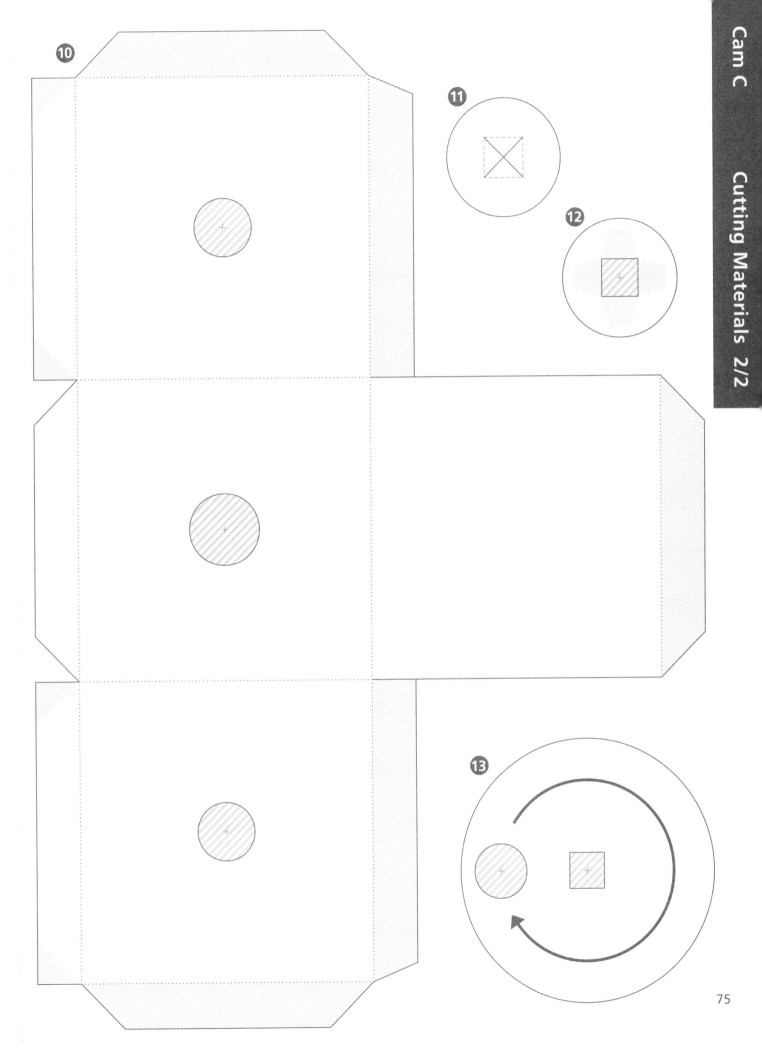

10

11

12

13

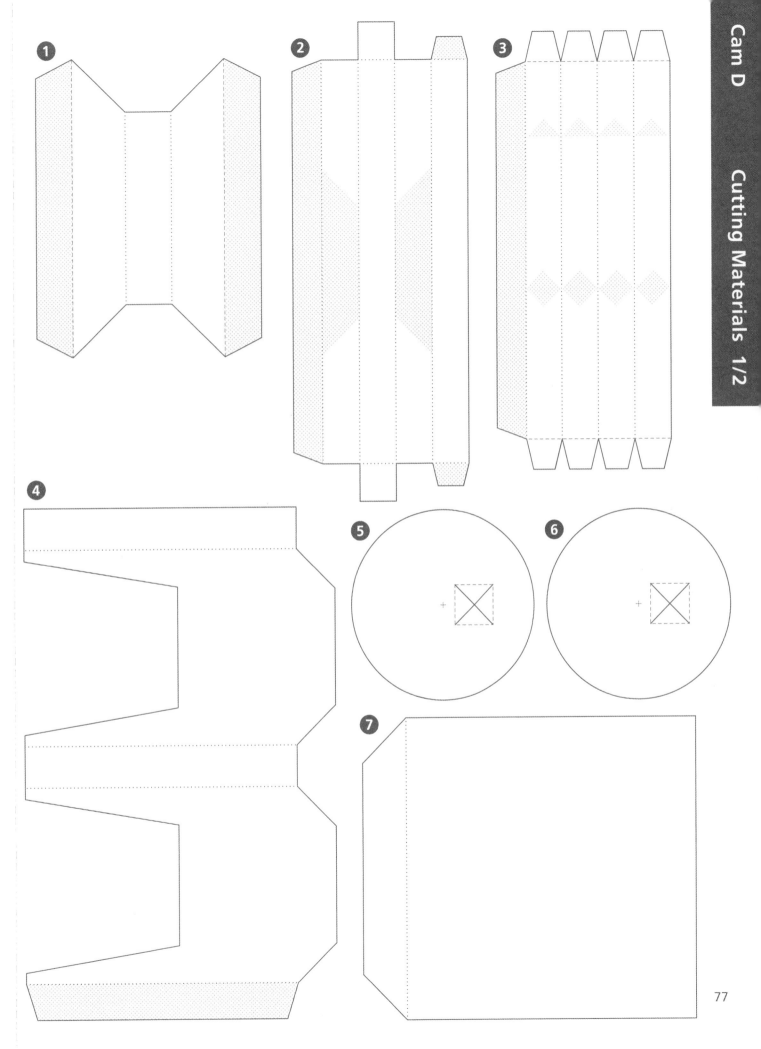

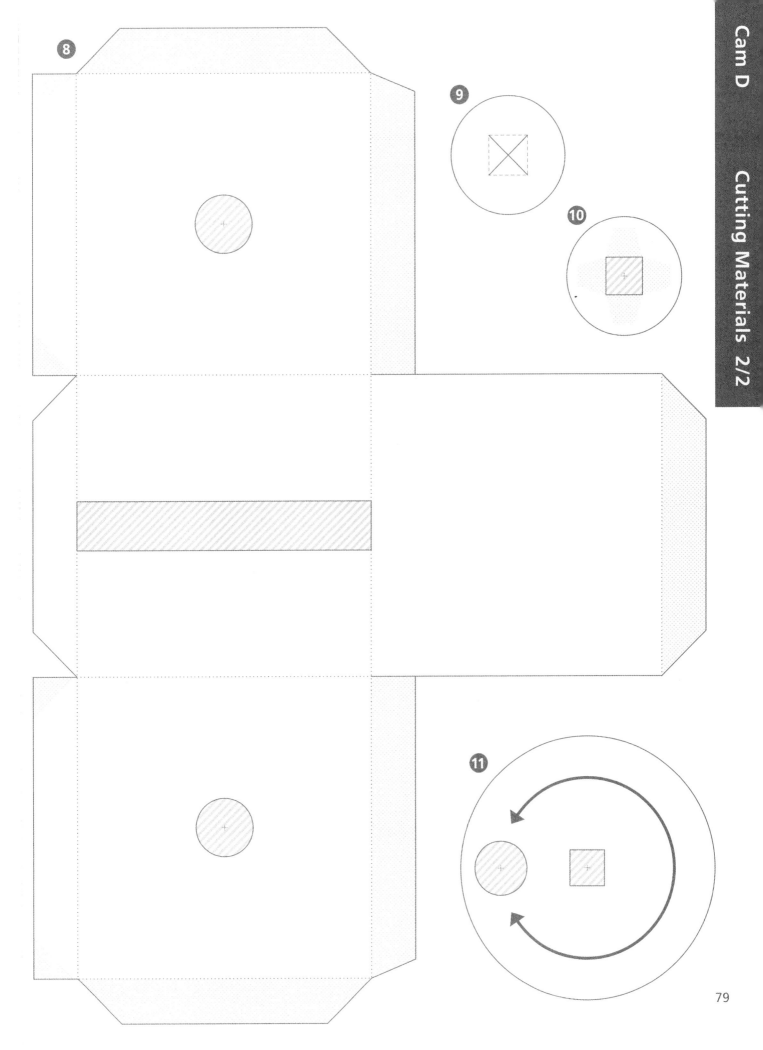

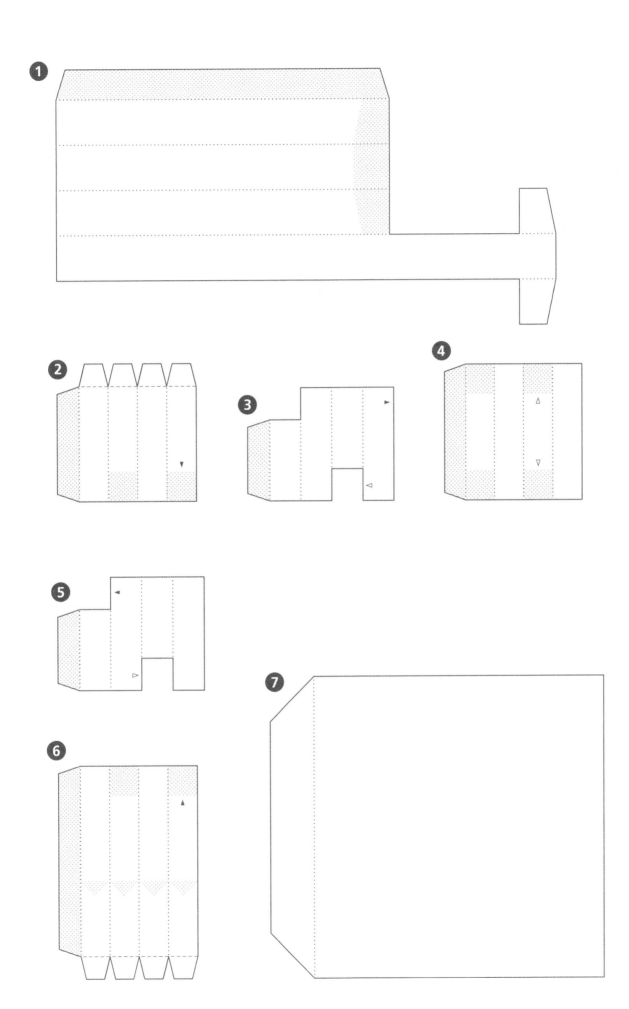

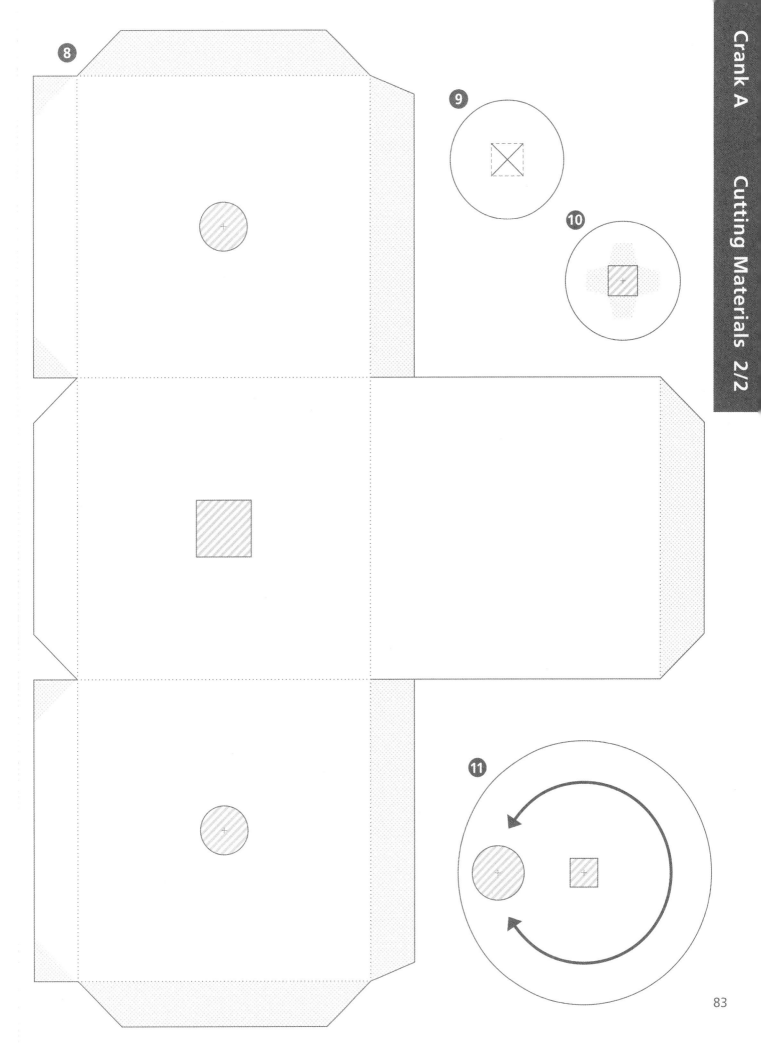

8

9

10

11

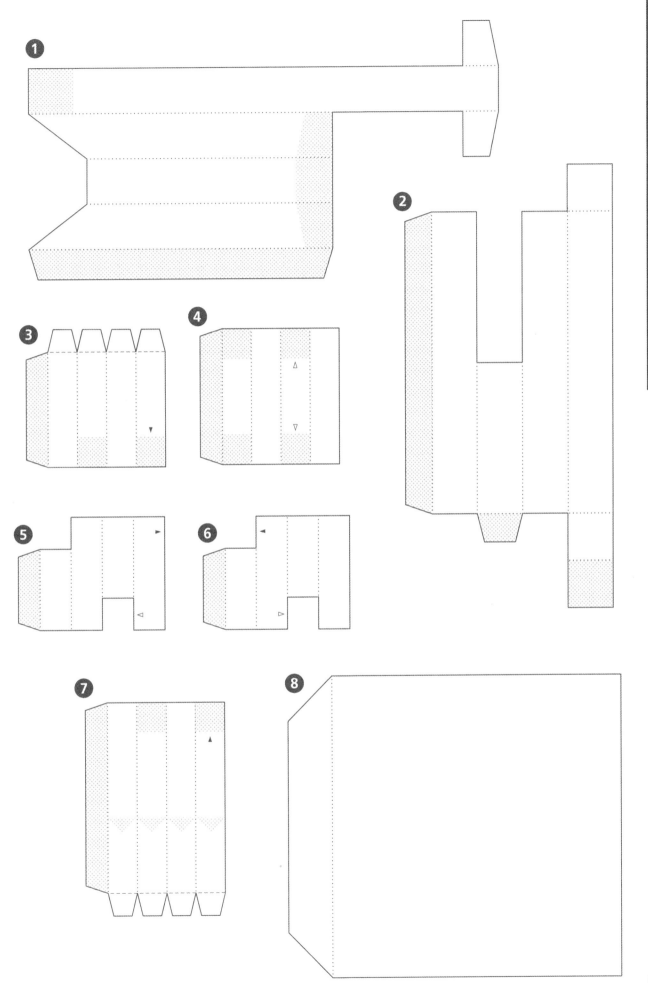

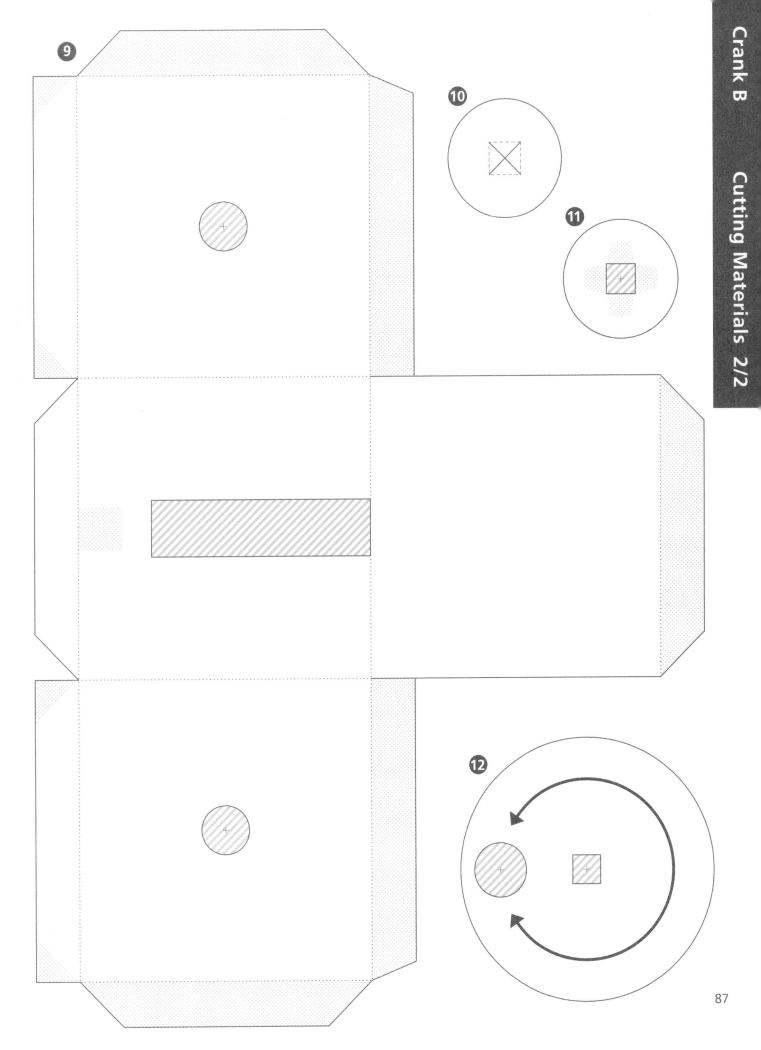

9

10

11

12

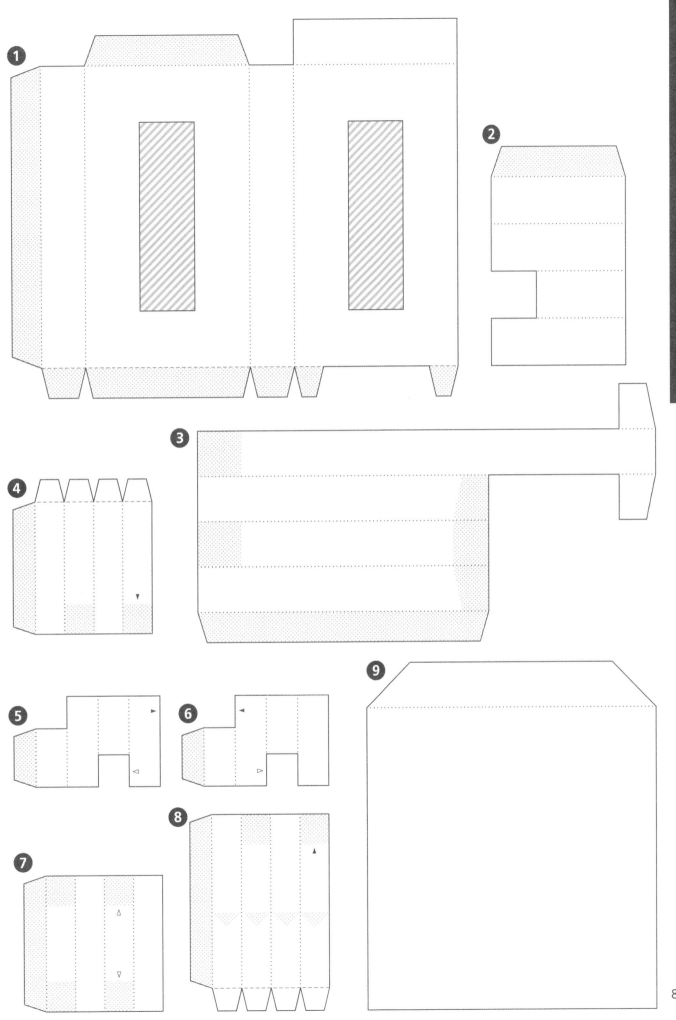

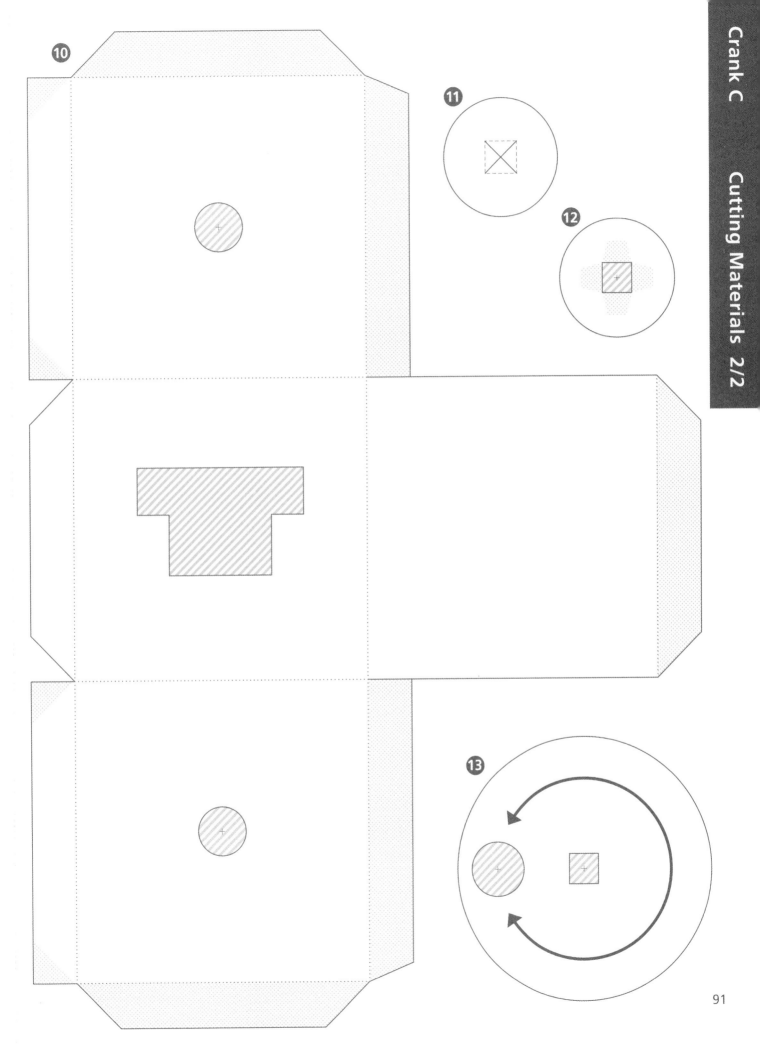

10

11

12

13

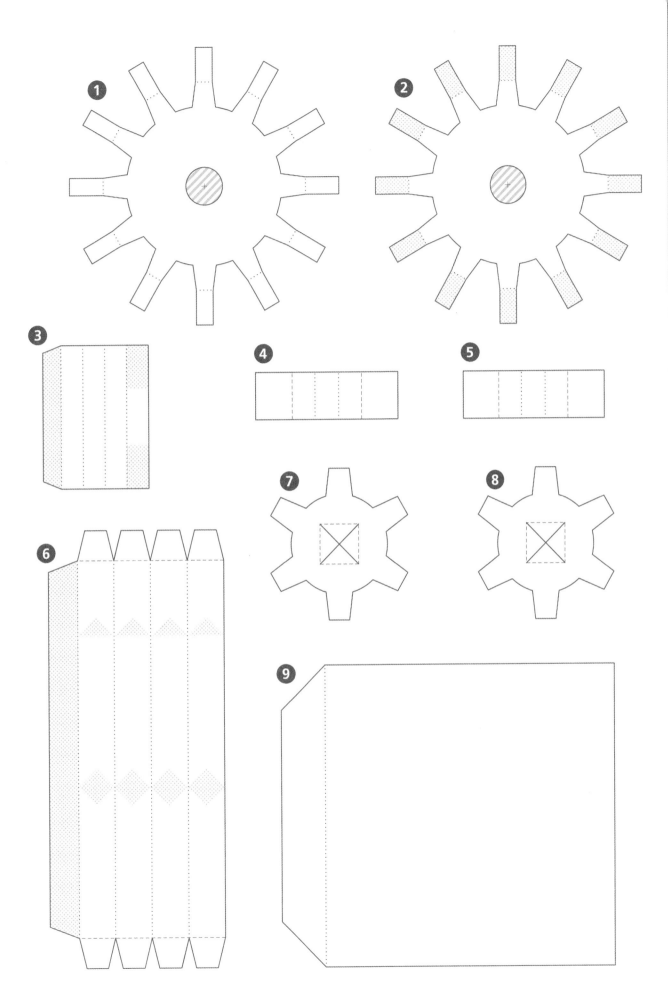

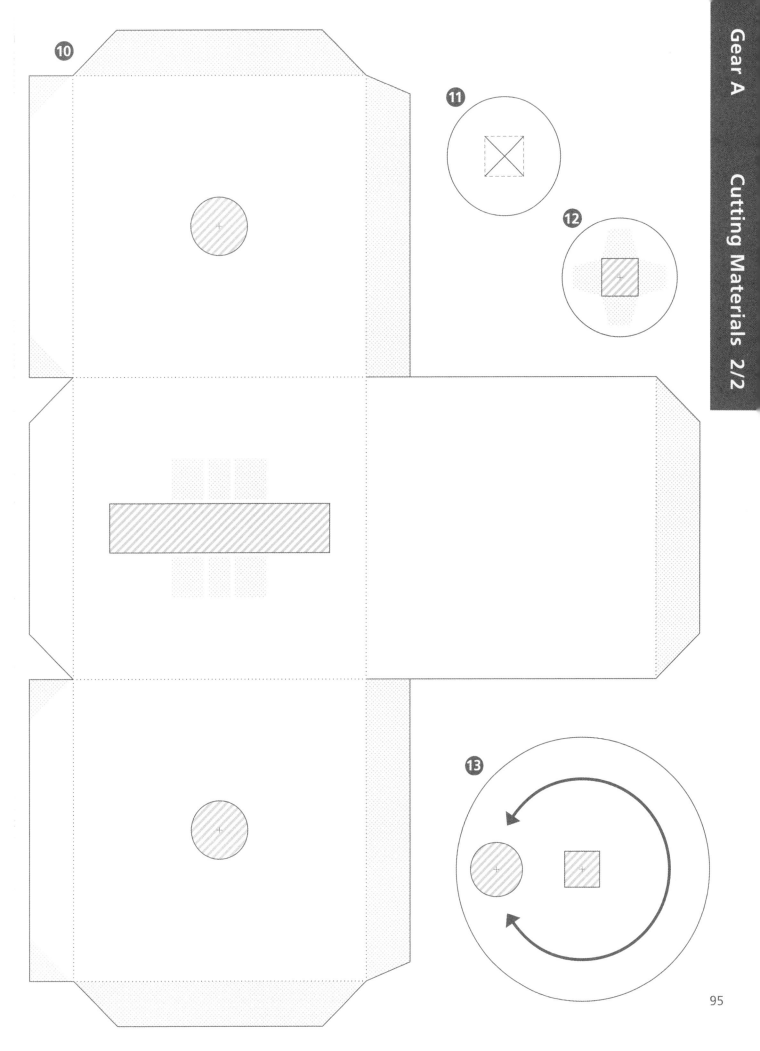

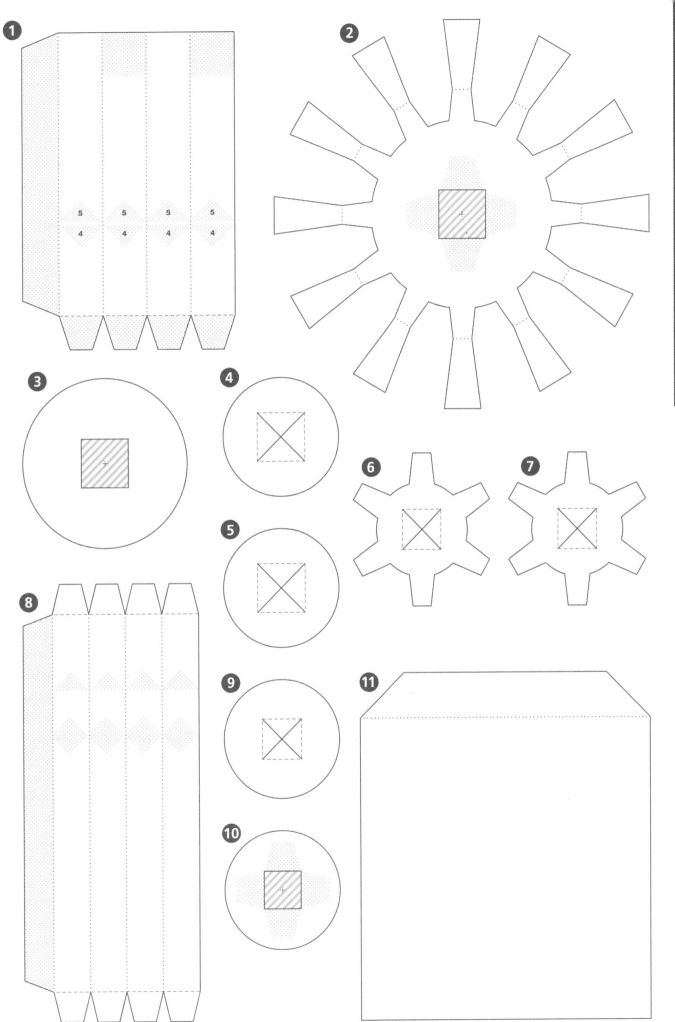

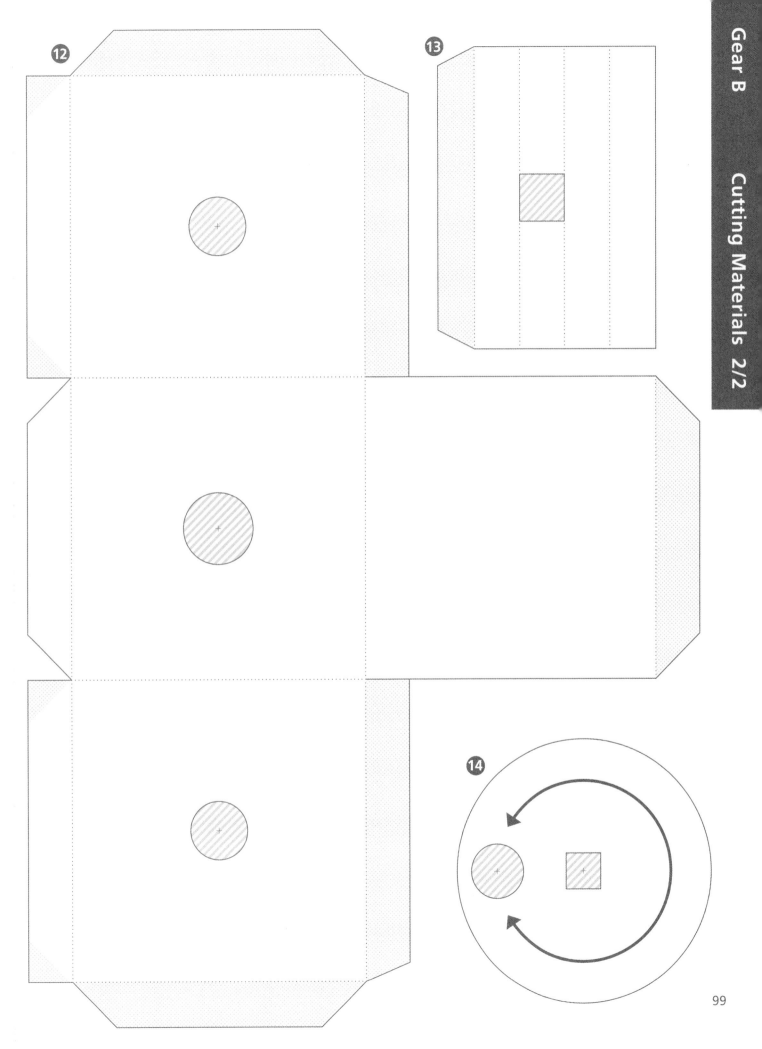

12

13

14

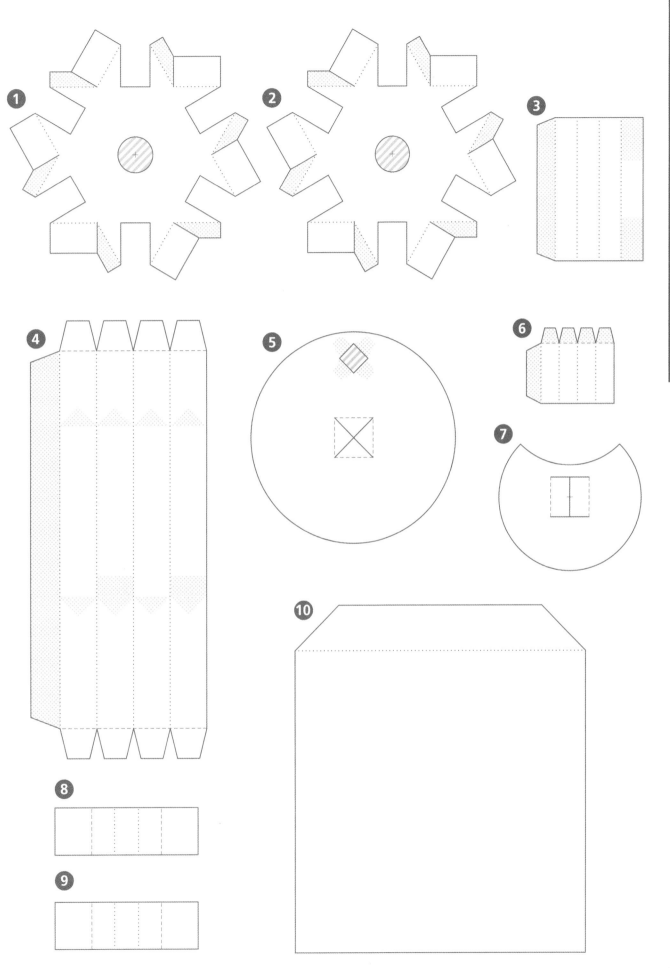

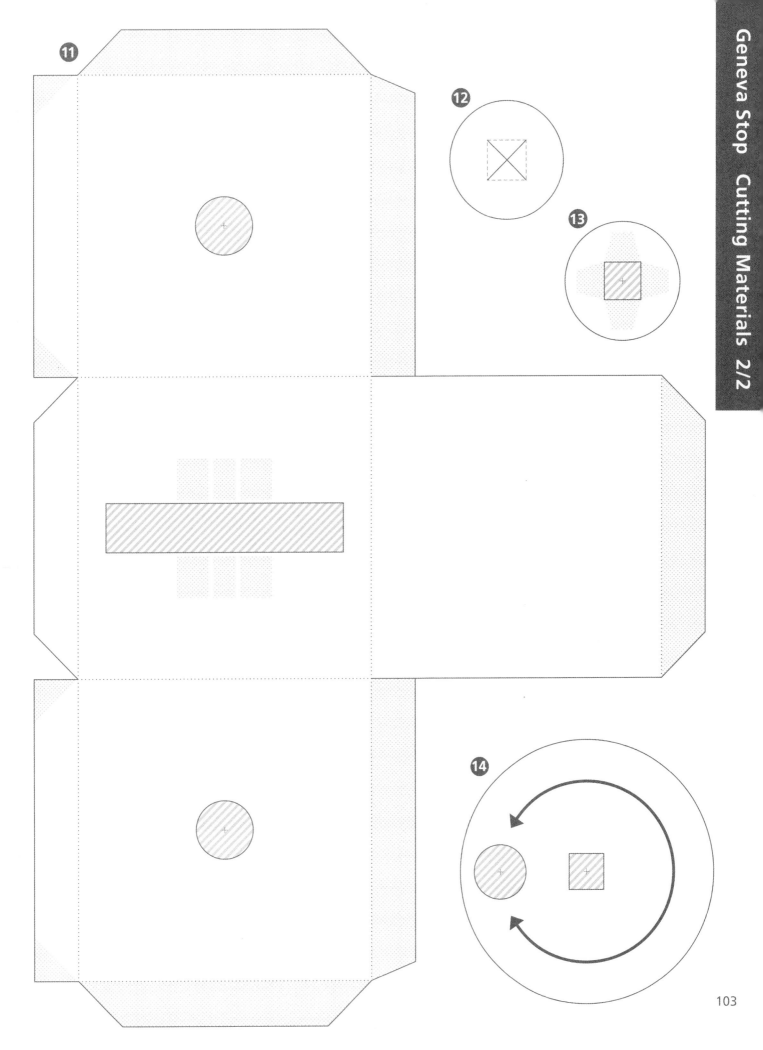

Seven of the ten basic karakuri models (Cam A, Cam B, Cam C, Cam D, Gear A, Gear B, and Geneva stop) can be joined to make a model connected with one handle.

1. Make each karakuri model mostly according to its instructions, but replace some of the parts in the model's cutting materials page with the parts below, indicated by number. Do not attach the handle to the axles. You should end up with separate models with square holes on the sides.
2. Place the models next to each other in the order you want, and insert the joining parts to connect them. No gluing is needed.
3. Build the insertable handle and insert it into the model on the end. You can try connecting the models in different combinations.

Cam A

For all 7 types

Joining parts x6

Insertable handle

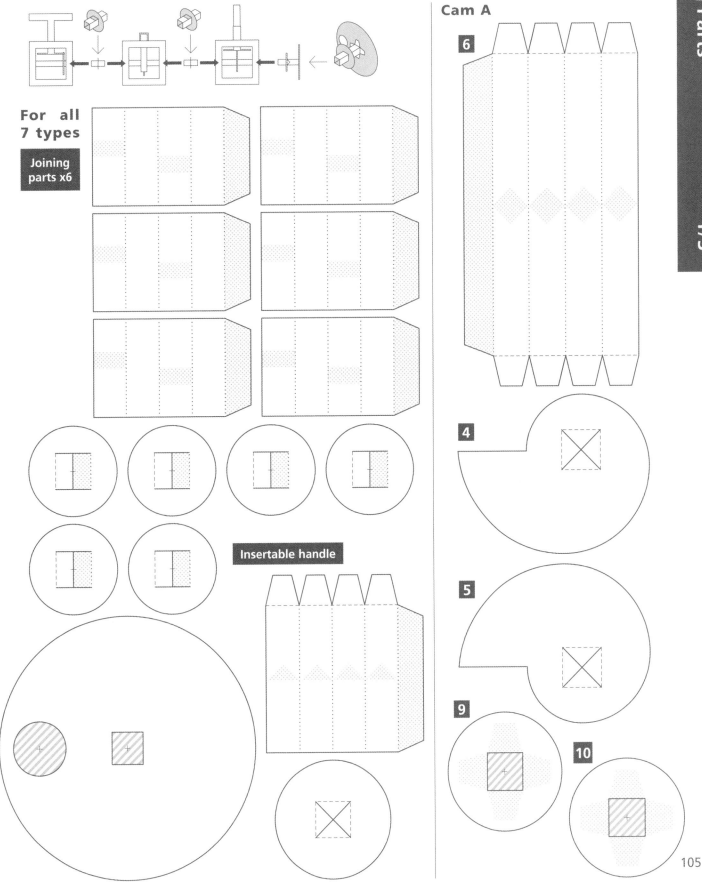

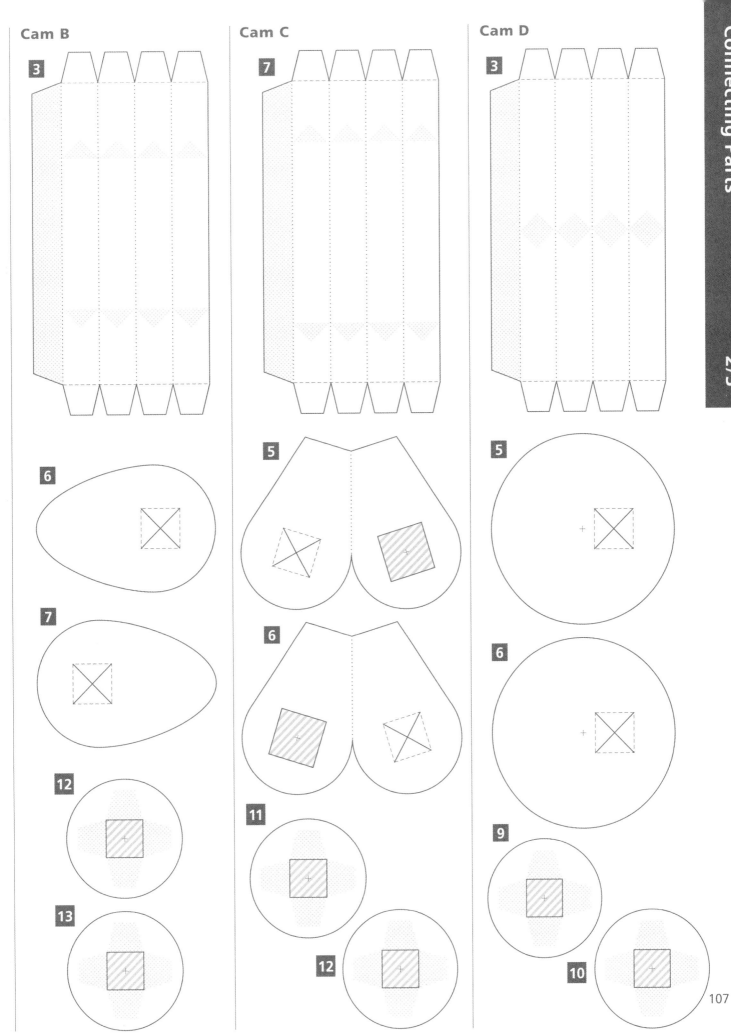

Cam B

Cam C

Cam D

107

Gear A

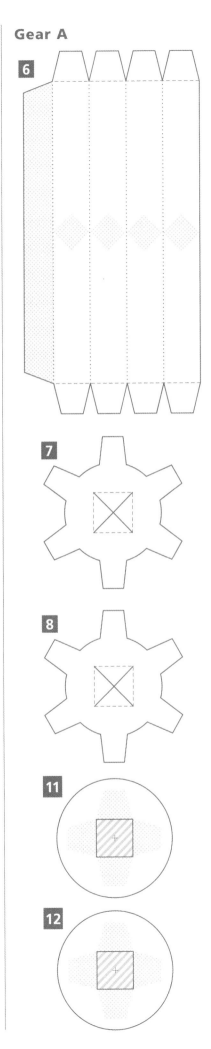

Gear B

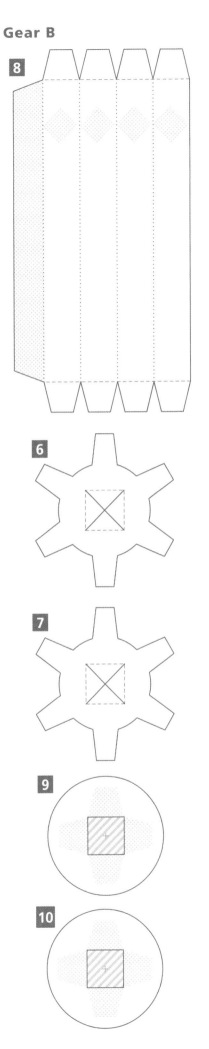

Geneva Stop

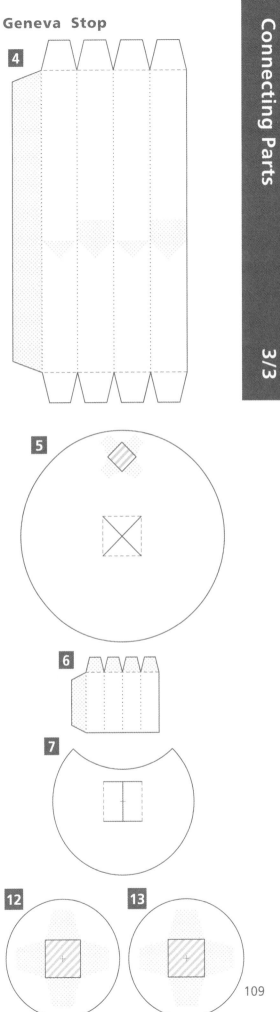

109

Fun Karakuri Models

 These pages are meant to be torn out of the book and cut to be used as building materials for the models.

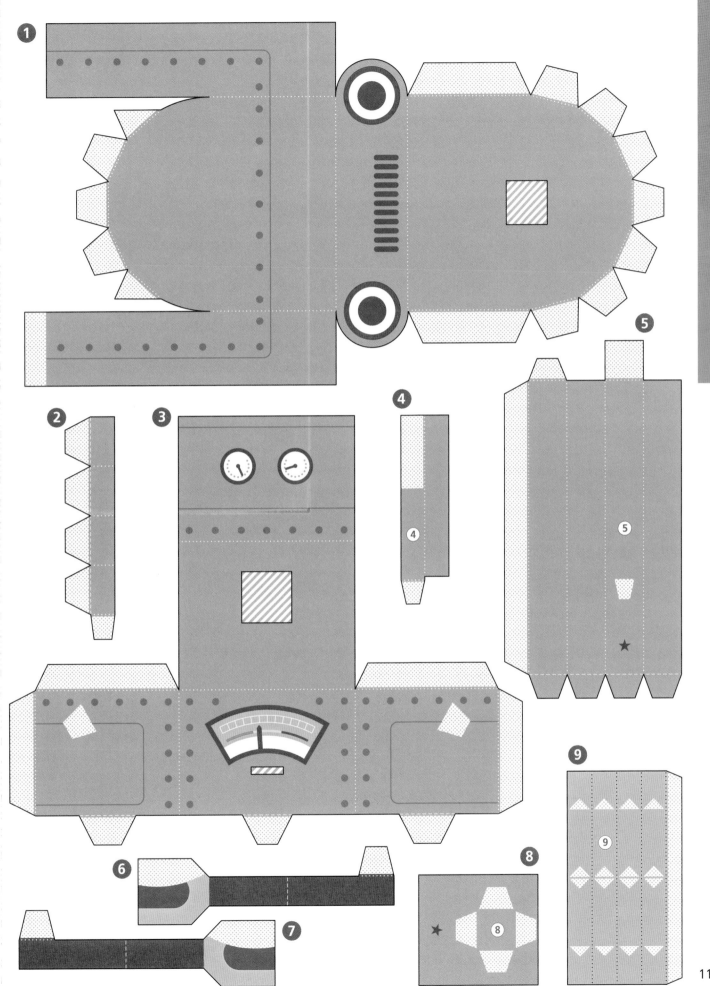

1

2

3

4

5

6

7

8

9

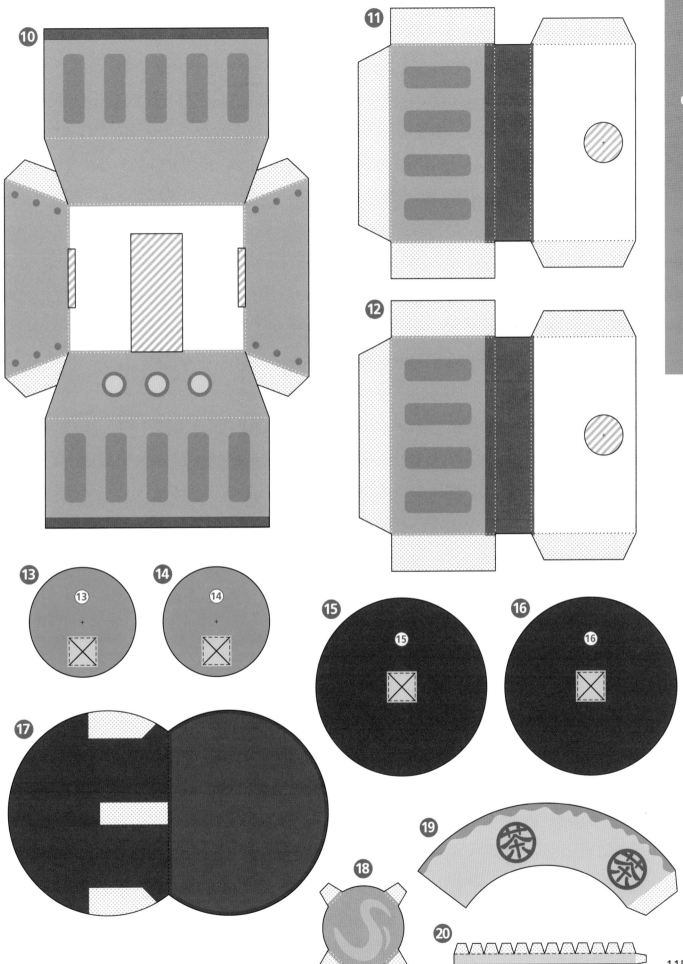

1

2

3

4

5

6

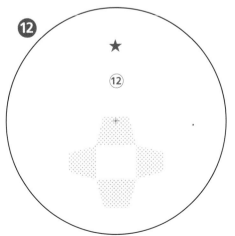

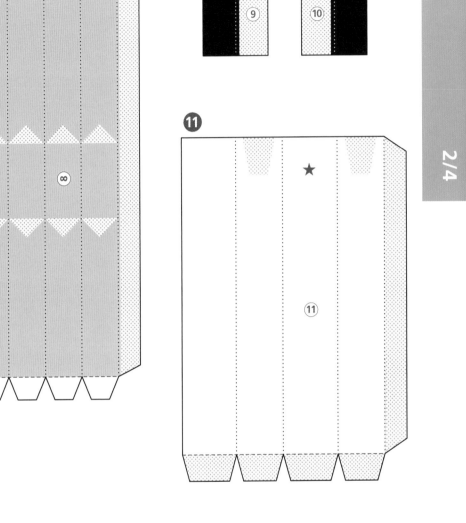

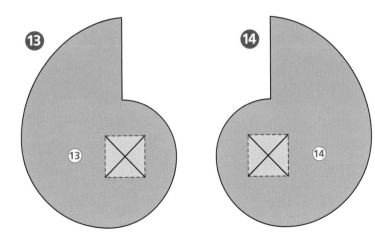

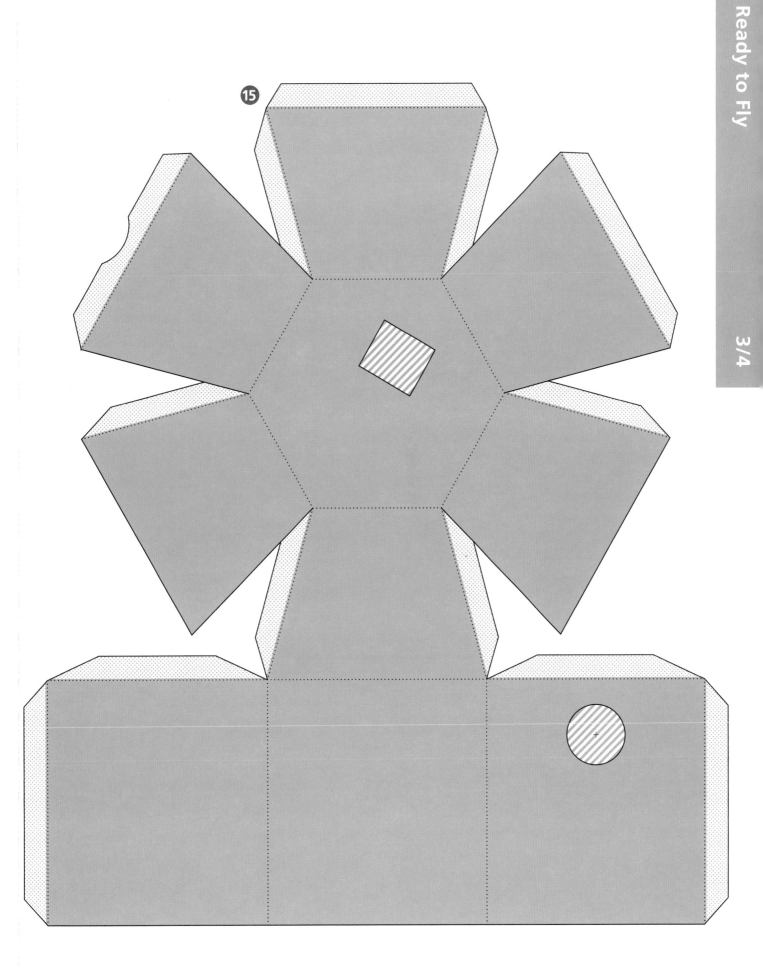

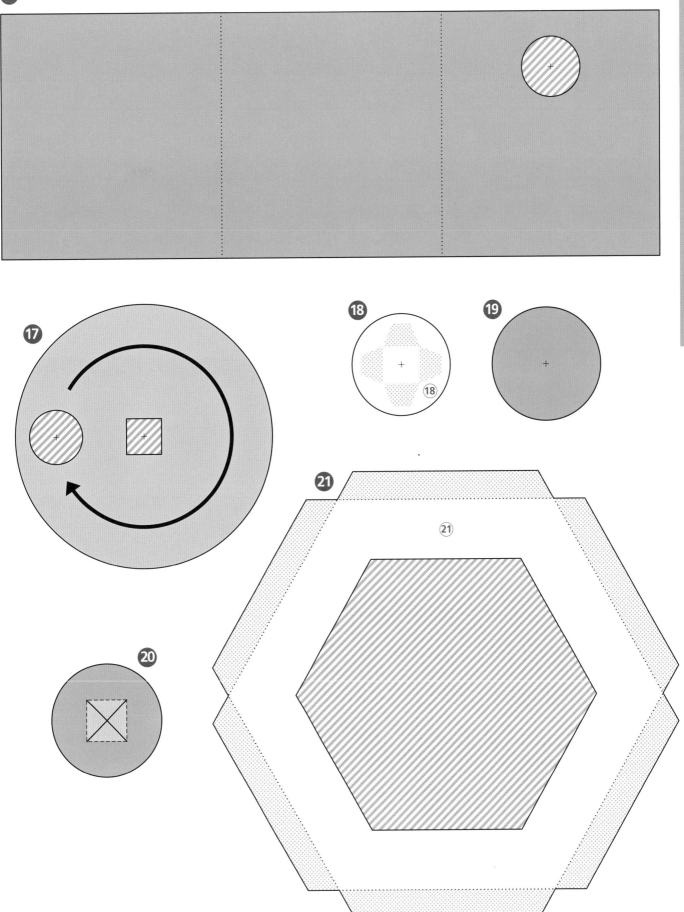

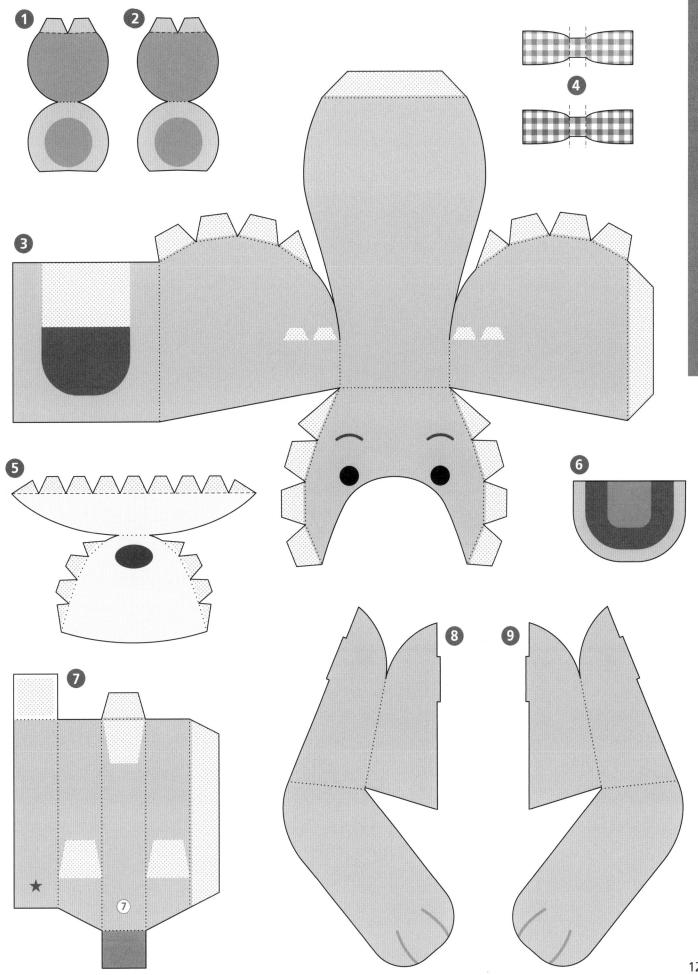

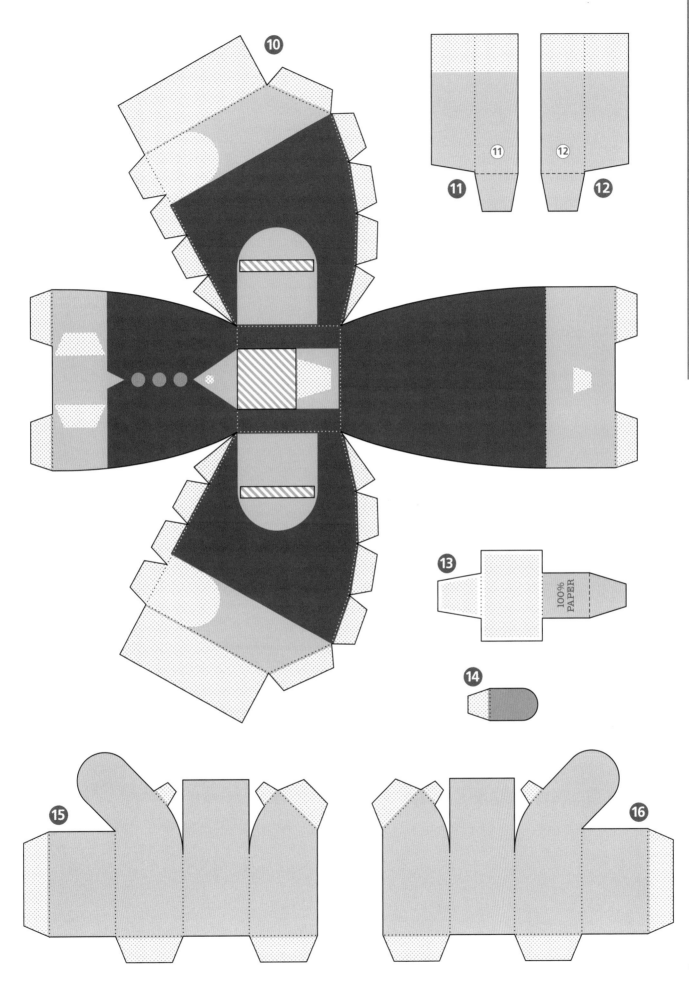

100%
PAPER

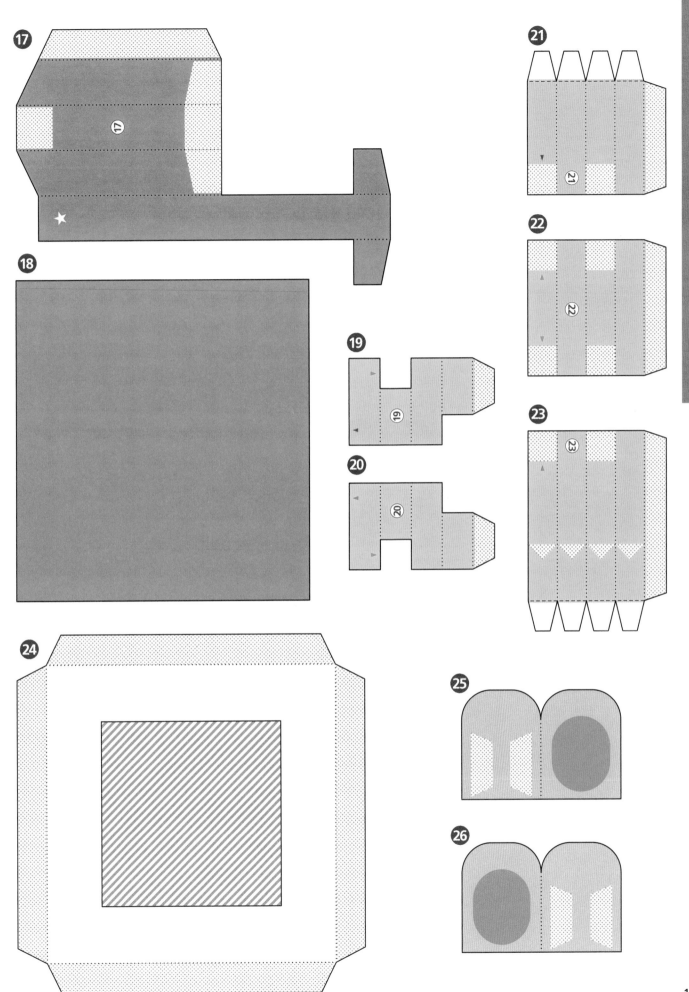

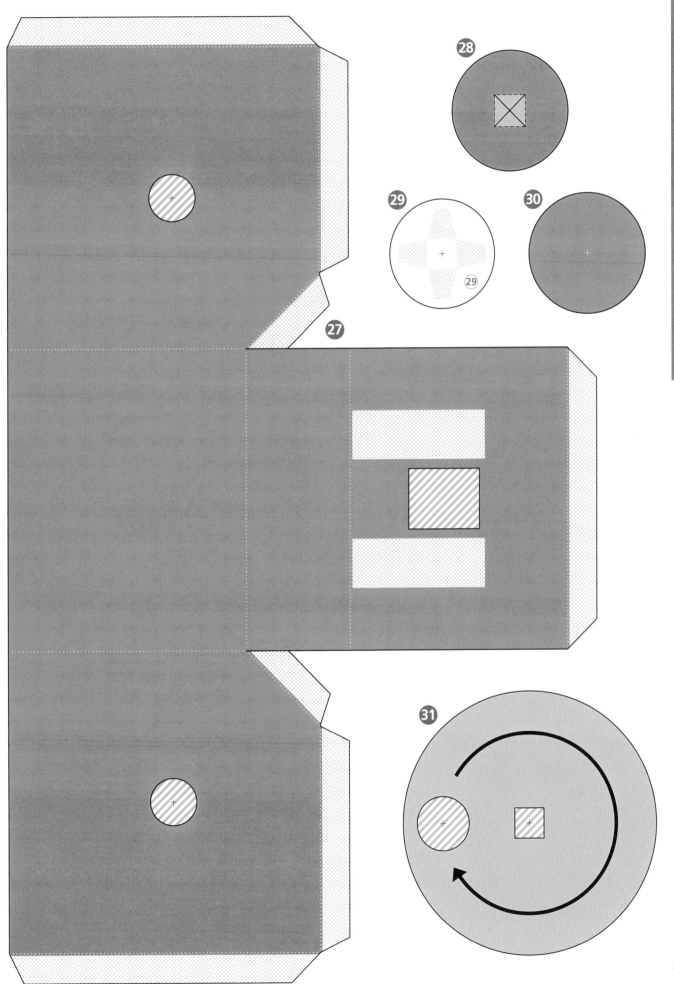

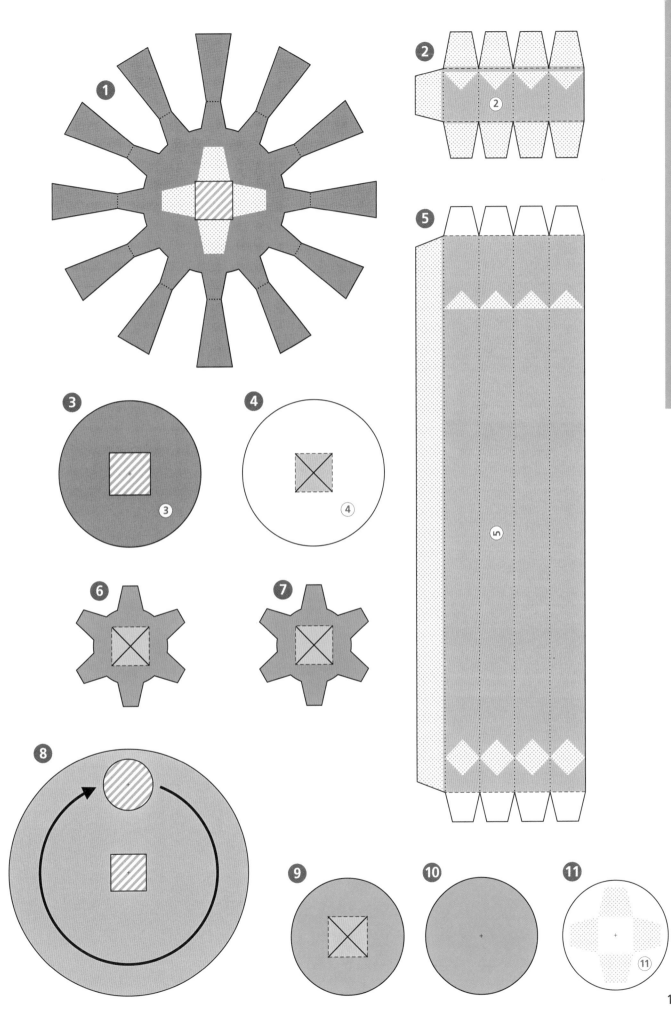

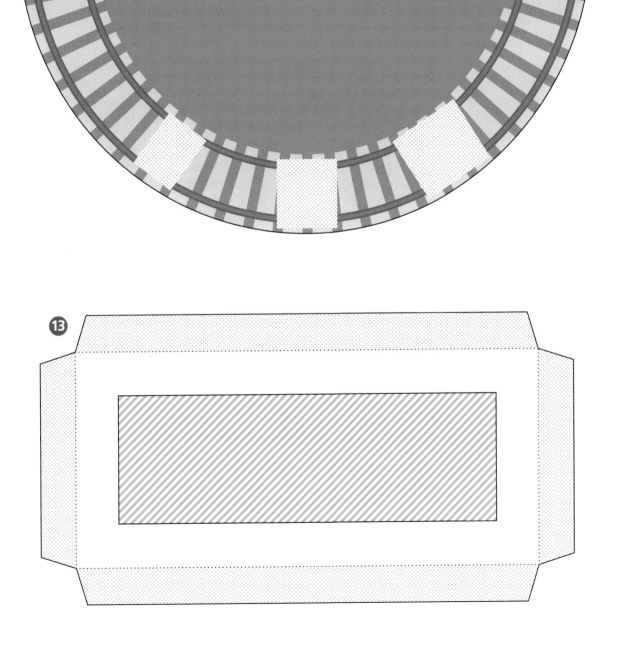

12

13

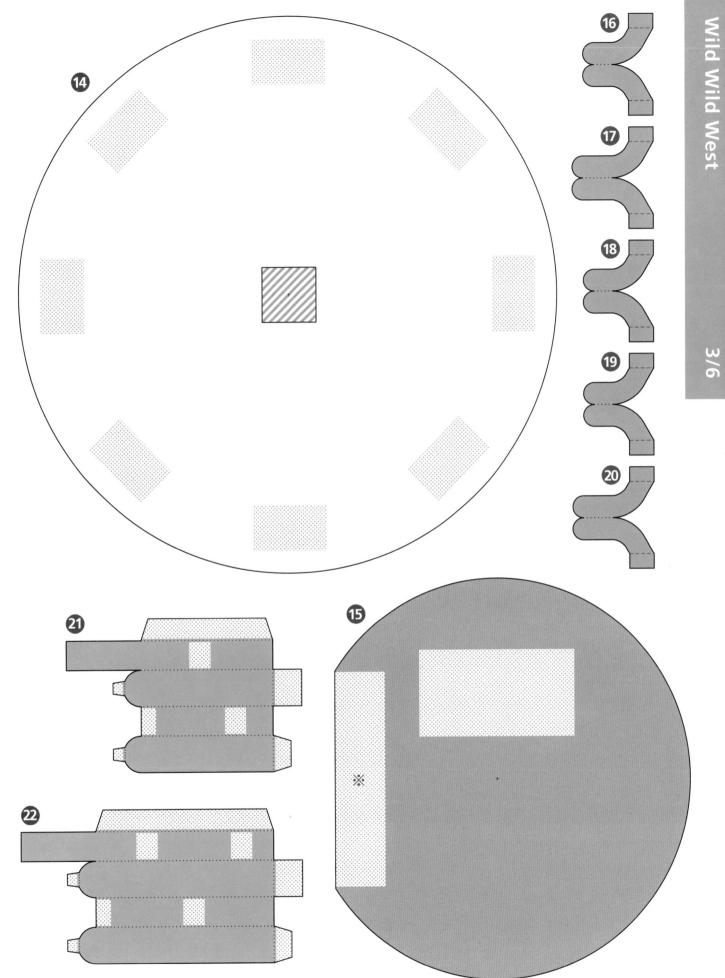

⑭

⑯

⑰

⑱

⑲

⑳

㉑

㉒

⑮

23

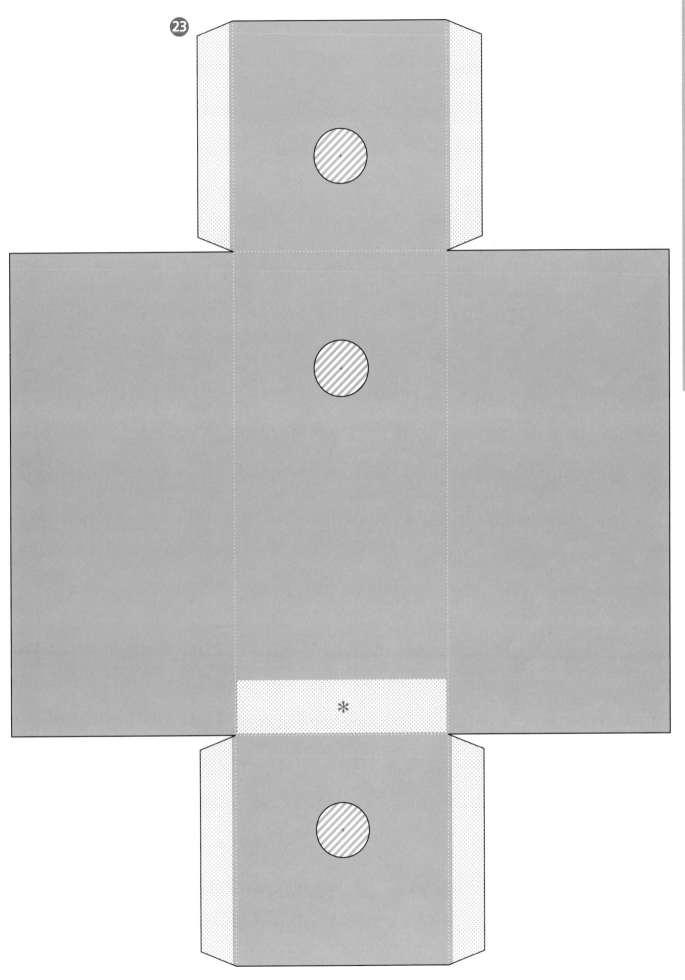

*

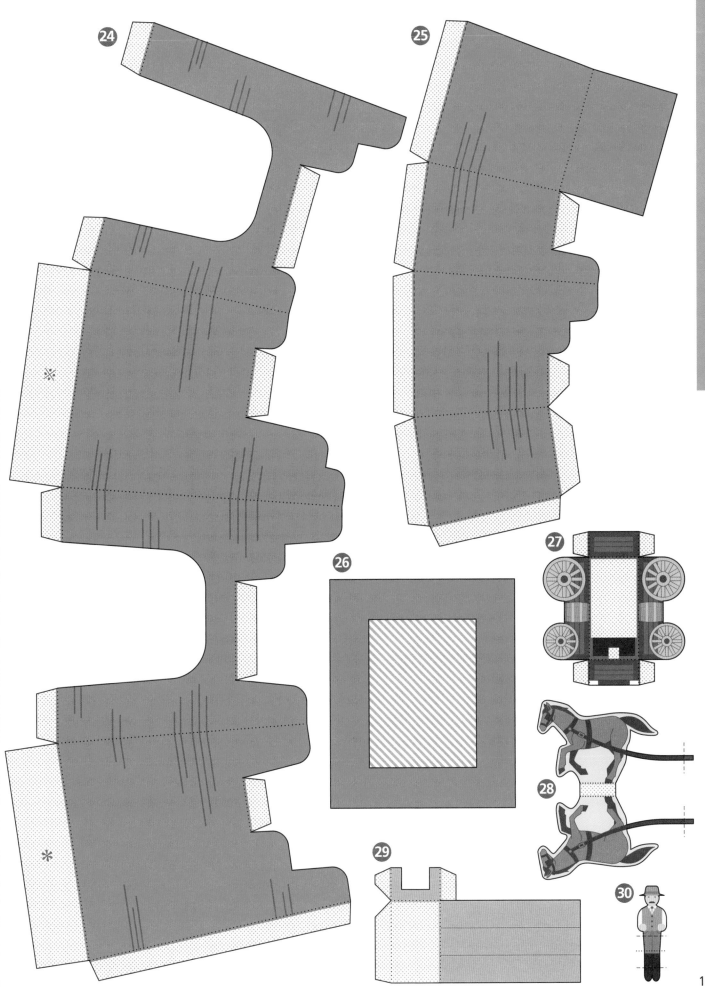

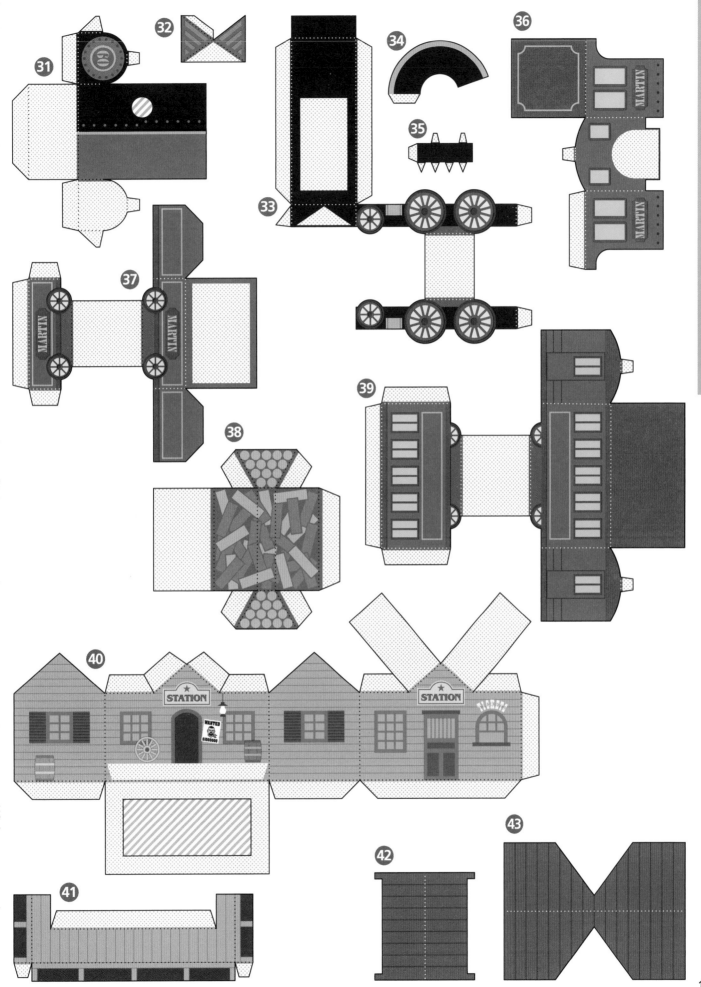

143

Contents

Dedication

To the bestest husband ever, Morgan Arkison. For teaching me the true value of sleeping in and pushing me to be more than I am today.

Acknowledgments

Two people were instrumental in bringing this book into being—Susanne Woods and Amanda Jean Nyberg. Our work on *Sunday Morning Quilts* inspired me to write this book. From that collaboration to this individual work, I couldn't have done it without them.

Thank-you to all the folks at Stash Books and C&T for believing that a quilt book can be more than a collection of patterns and that words can inspire as much as pictures. Speaking of pictures, a giant Zombie Underpants Screech for Kate Inglis, the style photographer.

This book would never have come into being without the support, cooking, play dates, photo sessions, and encouragement of my dear friends in the community around me. I've found my home, and it is because of them.

The patience of and cheerleading by my family are what got me through the sleepless new-baby nights. But next time I will listen to them when they suggest that I keep my plate clean for a little while. (But only in the short term.)

Finally, thank-you to all my readers and the quilters who continue to inspire me with their questions, interpretations, design, and help.

Introduction

Without a doubt, I am a color person. I need it around me, filling me with energy and smiles. I crave it when I'm surrounded by too much white. Put me in a beige home, and I will sit by the one pillow or photograph that has color in it, just to feel its vibrancy.

When people come to our house for the first time, there is always a bit of exclamation at the colors on the walls, the floor, the furniture. I'm sure there is a lot of wonder at how we can live with so much color. The answer is easy— we don't know how not to.

It isn't just that I'm a quilter either. I was the one who picked the brightest comforter when choosing bedding for my dorm room. I sought out rental apartments that allowed me to paint the walls. Basic black was never a concept my wardrobe understood. My obsession with color started long before my obsession with fabric.

Thankfully, I married a man who also relishes being surrounded by color. That, or he doesn't care that much and lets me take the lead. And my kids have obviously inherited this love of color. This means I can pile quilts in every room; paint my walls red, turquoise, or orange; or set the table with pink dishes without anyone complaining.

While I wouldn't change a single color in my life, there are times when even I need a little respite. Like a calm spot on a busy quilt, my eye and my soul need a place to rest in order to really appreciate everything.

That's where low-volume fabrics come in.

The white or light base of low-volume fabrics, combined with a colorful or graphic punch, is enough to keep visual interest without resorting to in-your-face color. There is still color and still boldness, but it is more like a stage whisper than a yell, more like an intermittent breeze than a Chinook wind.

My enthusiasm for low-volume fabrics can be linked to two clear inspirations. Malka Dubrawsky, of A Stitch in Dye fame, introduced me to the concept a few years ago. Malka is well known for her bright, graphic, hand-dyed fabric and improvisational use of color in sewing and quilting. But one day she shared a project that was a direct departure from her usual bright palette. To quote Oprah, it was an "A-Ha" moment for me.

I even had some of these low-volume fabrics around—I was obviously drawn to them without intention. In time, my collection grew.

I dabbled with using these patterns as background, in lieu of stark white. Then I made a scrap quilt for *Sunday Morning Quilts*, aptly named *Sunday Morning*. After that, there was no turning back—I was hooked on low-volume fabrics.

Just as I was finishing that scrappy quilt, we entered the final stages of an endless basement renovation. It's a basement, so it isn't exactly filled with light. To compensate, we added the biggest windows we could and agreed on white walls. The two bedrooms—one, the master, and the other, my studio/guest room—would get the most light. I had romantic visions of light and snuggles and pops of color.

Canada is a winter country, but it is also a light-filled place: long, long summer days and winter lights augmented by the bluest of skies and the whitest of snow on the ground. We wanted to channel that light in our new space, partly because it fits with our design preferences of late. And, well, because it is a basement.

Low-volume fabrics fit in this plan because they indeed channel the light, not only in their light/white base, but in their energy as well. It is impossible to see a stack of low-volume fabrics and think drab, dull, or lifeless. They inspire a bit of peace and a lot of quiet energy.

A Month of Sundays—Family, Friends, Food & Quilts is not the typical quilt book. I wanted to inspire more than just quilts in creating this book. Like the low-volume fabrics profiled in all the projects, this book is meant to inspire quiet energy. Embracing the spirit of the Sunday afternoon stroll, cloud watching, and painting with your children are all a part of that energy.

Built upon the four themes of *Relax*, *Eat*, *Shop*, and *Explore*, this book takes you through some personal journeys, while providing ideas to get you started on your own weekend explorations. I want you to sit and enjoy reading this book first, then go grab your fabric to create.

The projects in the book are based on the four themes, and all feature low-volume fabrics. All are inspired by the ideas discussed, but that doesn't limit them to weekends or low-volume fabrics. The patterns are straightforward and designed for the confident beginner and seasoned sewist. Many are precut friendly too. Nothing comes without some work, but hopefully this work is both exciting and restful, just like a perfect Sunday afternoon.

Turn It Down

Definitions and Tips on Using Low-Volume Fabrics

"BUT IT'S GOT ELEVEN!"

That famous line from the cheesy, over-the-top parody *This Is Spinal Tap* is all about volume. If a stereo has eleven, then turn it up. For many of us quilters and fabric lovers, this line is equally appropriate. The more color the better; the more saturated that color, even better.

Like every good sound system though, choosing fabrics for projects is more about the quality of the sound than the overall volume. You want it to pump, yes, but you also want to be able to hear the lyrics and the bass at the same time. Great quilt design can get lost in a sea of bright, saturated fabrics. When everything is bold (loud), then you see (hear) nothing.

This chapter is about the basics of using low-volume prints in your projects. When you turn down the volume, maybe to a four instead of an eleven, you can see different design notes, focus on the graphic nature of the fabric itself, and even hear what the maker was saying. The songwriter will now get as much appreciation as the guitar player or drummer.

What Makes a Quilt Low Volume?

In low-volume prints, the white/light base is generally the predominant color of the print. However, this concept can be reversed—the print may have a color for the background with a dominant white design. In this case, the print would still read as light. The print can be any scale or style—from boldly graphic lines and dots to florals and novelties—but without a graphic element, you essentially have a white-on-white or beige-on-beige fabric.

Low-volume quilts have a softer feeling than the high-volume ones. The mood, the tone, and the intensity of the quilt are more relaxed. Color, value, and scale/visual texture are all instrumental in achieving this result.

The primary characteristic of low-volume quilts revolves around contrast—low-volume quilts (softer) have less contrast than high-volume (or louder) quilts. This applies to color, value, and scale or visual texture.

Color Still Matters

When you turn down the volume, you still need to think about the elements of good design, including color, to make a project work.

Typically, when we talk about color, the color wheel comes out, and terms like *saturation*, *hue*, *tint*, and *tone* get thrown around. When you are working with low-volume fabrics, these properties of color become even more important.

SATURATION

Saturation is a reflection of the intensity of a color, or how much pigment there is to the color. For example:

Light pink	vs.	Fuchsia
Sage	vs.	Emerald green
Robin's egg	vs.	Cobalt

In low-volume fabrics, the colors can be saturated or less saturated. If the print is saturated with a predominant light background, it still reads as low volume.

TINTS, TONES, AND SHADES

Tints are created when white is added to a color, tones are created when gray is added, and shades are created when black is added. Using tints, tones, and shades greatly increases the pool of fabrics to choose from, especially when you want to keep the volume low while still making vibrant quilts.

When describing the tint, tone, or shade of a fabric, take into account both the fabric's print and background. Not all whites are created equal, for example—some will be brighter than others, and some will have tone.

Why Scale Is Important

An easy way to pick fabric for a quilt might be to use the multiple colors of one print available in a fabric line. But when you finish the quilt, it feels flat, like something is missing. If all the prints in a quilt are the same size, there is no variety of scale—kind of like a pop song that might be catchy but gets boring quickly because it is nothing but the same words and music repeated over and over again.

With the softer nature of low-volume fabrics, scale matters almost more than anything. Having similar-colored backgrounds in almost all of your fabrics means that the scale of the prints—the visual texture—becomes extremely important. The changes in scale from large to small and back again provide movement and strong design to a low-volume project.

A good line of fabric includes a variety of colors, patterns, and scales. For example, there could be a main large-scale floral print; several floral prints in a smaller scale; some very small, scattered flowers; and a few fabrics with dots or lines—all in several colorways. This variety of scale helps make for a more interesting design, even if you do use only a single fabric line for your quilt.

Value

Good use of value (how light or dark a fabric is) is as important when using low-volume fabrics as it is with any other type of fabric. Even more so, perhaps, because the value differences are less dramatic. Without variations in value, the design will be lost. As with scale, if all your fabrics are similar in value, the different shapes within the quilt design will be indistinguishable.

The colors in the fabric affect the value, as do the density and scale of the print design. Some fabrics will have a more sparsely printed design as compared with others; with white or light backgrounds, this affects the value. A densely printed design will generally read darker than a sparsely printed one.

When you make a quilt with similarly valued fabrics, expect a very quiet energy in the final project. It will be softer around the edges than a high-contrast project. This can be a design consideration. There are times when the quilt pattern needs high contrast, and times when a lighter touch works just as well. The important thing is to pay attention to value and scale—the visual texture—to finish the quilt with your design and energy goals in mind.

Evaluating Value

Here are two ways to evaluate your value and scale variations to determine whether or not they provide contrast.

NAKED-EYE TEST

Put two or more fabrics side by side. Squint. Can you easily see the differences between the fabrics, or do they look similar? Pay attention to the background color and value, as well as the type and density of the print or pattern. If their values and scales are similar, they will tend to blend together.

If you are struggling to see differences or similarities, or if you simply want to confirm your conclusion, try the black-and-white test.

BLACK-AND-WHITE TEST

With a digital camera or camera phone, take a photo of your fabrics side by side. Some cameras allow you to set your camera to black and white before you even take the picture. If you can do this, then do so before you snap the photo. Otherwise, the majority of basic photo-editing software packages have a way to convert photos into black and white. If you don't have a digital camera, photocopying fabric in black and white will also work.

After your image is in black and white, the grayscale image shows you nothing but value. Fabrics that look different when viewed with the naked eye may appear almost identical in black and white.

This test will confirm your naked-eye test or send you to look for more fabric. It might seem like an extra step, but it is worth the effort to make your project sing.

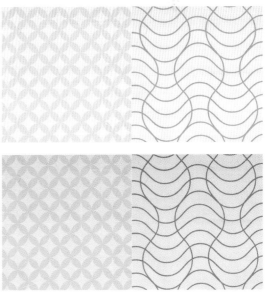

Fabric with similar value and scale

Fabric with contrast of value and scale

Background Choices

The safest bet when picking a background fabric for any low-volume project is a white solid. There is absolutely nothing wrong with that, but it isn't your only choice—it's just the safest.

Many fabric manufacturers that produce solid fabrics also produce a small range of white or cream solids. Picking a white background fabric is easier than picking the perfect white paint. For one, there are fewer choices, and two, you can hardly go wrong.

You can also try other colors, ranging from the palest of pinks or blues to creams or grays. Changing the background color can change the quilt's entire look, so audition a few different options.

Low-volume prints are made on a variety of background colors—some will be bright white, while others will be light grays, warm beiges, or creams. Using a variety of background fabrics in a quilt is a great way to avoid any worry about how the background will work with your prints.

Your background choices change the quilt's energy. Go with a single solid, and the quilt will feel calmer. Pick a brighter white for a quilt with more punch. Try mixing up your background fabrics in a single quilt, even if the pattern calls for only one fabric. And remember that your seamlines add another design element, more so than with brighter fabrics. So many options!

Showcase Your Quilting

Remember, in quilts with a lot of neutral space—where the design pops in a sea of a neutral background—the quilting will really stand out. Use this opportunity to play with and showcase the quilting.

Turn Up the Volume Variations

All the projects in this book can easily be made with other fabric choices. Each quilt pattern includes suggestions on how you might turn up the volume on the design.

Relax

Whether you are throwing rocks in a pond or sharing a beer with a friend, what's important is slowing down to enjoy the moment. Ultimately, that's what relaxation is about—forgetting about stress by focusing on something right in front of you.

When I started making quilts, this is what it was about. To keep from making mistakes and hurting myself, I had to concentrate on the quiltmaking. That meant no thinking about grad school papers or my boring job reading legislation—only the quiltmaking, only in the moment.

True relaxation comes from living a real life and taking the time to enjoy the thrill that comes with what's here right now, such as a perfectly skipped rock bouncing across the water.

Shhh...

There is a moment on a vacation when the body and brain click off. In that moment, after days of reading, swimming, hiking, shopping, or eating too much, you don't sleep in, the book languishes beside you, and you think you might actually be bored. In reality, however, that isn't boredom—it's relaxation. You've finally arrived at the moment where the stress is gone. Of course, it usually happens the day before the vacation ends!

We don't all have the luxury of time and money for do-nothing kinds of vacations. Without breaks from real life, though, we'll go bonkers. Enter the weekend—often filled with errands, housework, obligatory family visits, and birthday parties. It can get hectic. But weekends can also be the time to relax, reveling in not having to face the workday, commutes, or soccer practice.

About the most indulgent thing I can do is nothing. It was this way long before I had kids, and now, with my kids running around, it is the epitome of luxury.

Lying about started for me when I was a surly teenager. Looking to avoid church, I pretended to be asleep on Sunday mornings. My parents, wanting to avoid an argument first thing in the morning, usually left me alone. I was often awake, so I would lie in bed and quietly read, quickly hiding my book when the footsteps indicated they were coming to check on me! Even after they left, I stayed in bed a little while longer, reveling in my teenage victory and peach-colored comforter.

Fast-forward to those days after university, in the throes of young love and disposable income. Weekend mornings were often spent in bed, not by choice, but because my body had no will to get up with the previous night's adventures clouding my brain. Even on the good days, however, I loved to lie in my sunny bedroom and do nothing more than enjoy the light and the company. In those days, I had a wild citrus and turquoise comforter.

Our first baby brought about lazy mornings with her snuggled between us. We reveled in her presence, despite the early hours. After months on bed rest, I actually didn't think I would want to lie about, family or not, but those mornings were precious. We brought her in when she woke to tickle, nurse, or otherwise fawn over her. With more kids, however, the mornings are far from relaxed, but we still find time to gather under our wedding quilt.

Regardless of the season, gathering to lie about is part of our family. In a small house with no chimney, Christmas morning is a brain-teaser for little girls. Santa now visits us just outside the bedroom. When the girls wake up, they race down the short hall, double-check the cookies to confirm that Santa did indeed arrive, then burst open the door to our room. We crowd in the bed, eating oranges and chocolate and investigating our gifts. There is bed jumping and wrestling and loads of cajoling to get us parents out of bed. So we throw aside a wintry quilt and get our day started.

My ideal day as a mother now includes loads of lie-about time. If I could, I would stay in bed, soaking in the morning sun with a weekend newspaper or captivating novel. I might even get a crossword puzzle started. People would bring me some tea and toast instead of me getting it for them. The indulgence of time spent in relaxation is the best gift anyone can ever give me.

Alas, I am a mother, a wife, a quilter, and more. Opportunities to lie about are very few and very far between. I take full advantage of every quiet cup of tea, every swing on the porch, and every morning where I don't have to be the first one to get out of bed. Those moments of peace are indulgent, yes, but they are also energizing. For every time you can turn away from the to-do lists, you can find the light that keeps you going; you can find inspiration to bring vibrancy to the other, not-so-quiet moments of life.

How can you grab moments or even whole afternoons of relaxation? I'll share with you how I take advantage of or even create the quiet spots in life. Be sure to bring the rest of your family with you, because the more they seek out the quiet moments, the more you will get. Embrace the ease of a Sunday afternoon with no yard work or birthday parties. Wrap your hands around a kid or a mug of coffee and indulge in moments of peace.

Stare at the Clouds

Throw your quilt on the ground and stare up. It isn't more complex than that. Pick out the dragons, butterflies, and Stephen Colbert shapes in the clouds. If there are no clouds that day, then watch for birds and airplanes.

Don't wait for the summer to do this. With a skylight or big window, you can do this all winter long. Park yourself in front of the light and watch. Wrap yourself in a quilt for extra indulgence.

The whole point is to just sit and be. Staring at the clouds is the easiest form of meditation around. When you are looking for the perfect shape, that's all you can think about. When you are doing it with a loved one, their physical presence is calming. When you are lying on a quilt, the warmth comes from the sun and your back. There is no dinner to make or project to finish; it's just you and the sky.

Harness the Wind

Cool breezes are for more than fluttering the lace curtains (though that is a fine purpose). The wind brings with it the promise of flying dandelion seeds, tangled hair, and color flying through the sky.

We can't all live near the ocean and spend our Sunday afternoons sailing, but we can fly a kite, hang a windsock, or blow on a pinwheel to bring the simple beauty of a breeze to our hands. Kids naturally flock to things that seem to move of their own volition. It's the flap and snap of fabric as the wind takes it. It's the secondary breeze from the movement. It's the color, the dance, and the simple energy of the wind.

A near perfect day for me would indeed involve the water and the wind cutting a boat through the deep blue of the Atlantic Ocean. There would be beer, friends, loads of laughter, and even a little fear. Alas, I live on the Prairies, and the only time I sail is when gracious friends take me out the moment I descend upon their dock. But I can put fabric to the wind and hang on to the breeze.

Puzzles

My father-in-law was a fiend for jigsaw puzzles. Not much of a TV watcher, he set up a table behind the couch so he could hang out with the family while he worked away on a puzzle and they watched TV. Not just any puzzle either—it was always something like a 5,000-piece, all-blue puzzle.

The act of searching for just the right piece (after the straight lines of the outside of a puzzle are completed) is a meditative act. For some, it's downright frustrating. For others, it is an opportunity for tension to fall away. And for more, it is simply a way to keep the eyes and hands busy while sitting. There is a reason that puzzles are often ongoing in hospital lounges, after all.

One of my favorite things about jigsaw puzzles is that anyone and everyone can work on them. No one owns the process. Set up a table where anyone can sit down and work on the puzzle, even to search for just one piece. Just five minutes of quiet contemplation, of letting your brain wander over the colors, has to be equivalent to a few minutes of meditation or a cup of tea. Better yet, bring your tea to the puzzle table.

Stolen Words

When the demands of the day with little ones are too much, we gather on the couch or, even better, on the porch swing, with a stack of books, the dog at our feet, and the stories of the world in our hands. I'm teaching my kids the pleasure of reading. We started before they could even hold a book themselves, and I hope it continues to the point that we can all spend afternoons poring over books on our separate chairs, dog-eared pages welcome.

Throw Rocks

We are fortunate to live near a reservoir. You can't swim in it, but you are allowed to sail, row, and play on the beaches. In our family, one of our simplest family activities is to go and throw rocks in the water. The handfuls that the girls chuck in the water make a not-so-quiet PLOP! PLOP! PLOP! as the rocks break the surface. We adults work hard to skip the not-actually-flat rocks.

We don't talk much as the rocks fly. It's an unexpected break from the city behind us and an uninterrupted view of the mountains beyond. Everyone is in quiet contemplation with the rote nature of the rock flinging.

Somewhat contemplative and ultimately pointless, rock throwing can be done just about anywhere—the beach, a stream, a puddle in the back alley, or the slough at the farm. Rocks plus water, that's all you need.

No rocks around? The same effect can be had from gathering pinecones, looking for four-leaf clovers, searching for sea glass, and picking out pretty fall leaves.

Catch Up

Friendships don't just happen. They need a spark first—a common interest, a shared joke, a random encounter. Then they need to be fueled; otherwise, they fizzle out. The best way to fuel that relationship is with conversation—a real, person-to-person conversation, where you can hear the inflections in the voice and see the blinks and tears in the eyes.

With time being so precious to every one of us, the opportunity to sit with a friend and chat is priceless. Whether it's coffee with another mom, Skype with another quilter, or wine with your neighbor, catching up with friends is one of the most relaxing things you can do.

When you gather with people, it's hard to multitask your thoughts. Sure, your hands can be wrapped up in crafty things, but you must personally be engaged in the conversation. Quilting, knitting, and crafting make it easy to talk over an activity. There is also a natural intimacy that comes when you catch up over something like quilting. There are no awkward pauses, only moments of concentration. Shared creativity invites secrets to be divulged.

Paper Quilts

Paper quilts are a lovely way to play with design and to get your younger ones involved in the art of quiltmaking. It is a low-stress way to engage the mind creatively. With paper, you can play, arrange, and design with no commitment. Like putting together a puzzle, it is at once mindless and captivating.

If you are already a scrapbooker, you likely have a bin of scrap paper around and piles of more gorgeous papers to work with. Not a scrapbooker? Then pull out the kids' construction paper and watercolor paintings and cut them up. Of course, you could also always go shopping …

SUPPLIES

- Paper scraps, kids' old art (the stuff you don't want to save), scrapbook papers

- Paper cutter and good paper scissors (Don't use your fabric scissors!)

- White foamcore board cut to 10″ × 10″ or more (but small enough to carry) or heavy white paper

- Glue (*optional*)

PREPARE

Trim your paper to a variety of sizes and shapes. Start with squares, rectangles, and triangles that can all work together.

For example, cut:

- Squares 1″ × 1″, 2″ × 2″, and 4″ × 4″

- Rectangles 1″ × 2″ and 2″ × 4″

- Triangles with the right angle sides cut to 1″ × 1″, 2″ × 2″, 1″ × 2″, and 2″ × 4″

PLAY

Spread your paper on the table or floor in a draft-proof area. This is not an activity for the porch on a breezy day!

Start arranging your papers in pleasing designs. Basic patchwork, half-square triangles, brickwork, or more! You don't actually have to create functional designs. Use the white of the background as part of the design if you'd like.

Keep your papers in a small box to keep the shapes together and not strewn all over the house when a door gets opened or a small child plays superhero.

If you love what you've done and don't want to forget the design, grab your camera or a gluestick!

View

|||||||||||||||||||||||||||||||||||||||||||||||||||||||||||||||||||||||||||||||||||||||||||||||||||||||||||||||||

Finished quilt: 42″ × 42″ | Made by Cheryl Arkison

Strip bundle and mini charm pack friendly

Once, in a design workshop, I played around with the softest of colors in a winter prairie theme: blues, grays, whites, and pale yellows. As the pile of scraps built up next to me, more inspiration hit. I thought of showcasing the same fabrics while playing with the concept of negative space. I've always liked the Japanese garden theme of a borrowed view. In this case, the scraps are a borrowed view of my quiltmaking process.

Cutting Instructions

PIECED BLOCK

- Cut a total of 64 squares 2½″ × 2½″.

- *OR* -

- For a random version, trim the scraps into rough squares and rectangles 2″–3″ × 2″–3″. You will need at least 64 pieces, but possibly more if your pieces are closer to 2″ × 2″.

BACKGROUND

Cut:

- 1 piece 19½″ × 42½″

- 1 piece 7½″ × 42½″

- 1 piece 16½″ × 7½″

- 1 piece 16½″ × 19½″

BINDING

Cut as needed for your preferred method of binding.

Some Assembly Required

Seam allowances are ¼″.

1. Place the small pieces in a basket or bowl next to your sewing machine. Give them a stir to mix them up.

2. Chain piece (page 137) the squares until you have 8 rows of 8 squares. If you are pressing the seams to one side, be sure to alternate the direction by rows so the seams nest when you sew together the rows. If making the random version, check the length of the rows once they are pressed. Add pieces until the length is at least 16½″.

3. Sew the rows together and press the seams open or in one direction. For the random version, make additional rows if necessary to create a square that measures at least 16½″ × 16½″.

4. Trim the block to 16½″ × 16½″, if necessary.

5. Sew the 16½″ × 19½″ background piece to the top edge of the pieced block. Sew the 16½″ × 7½″ background piece to the bottom edge of the pieced block. Press toward the background.

6. Sew the 19½″ × 42½″ background piece to the left edge of the center section. Sew the 7½″ × 42½″ background piece to the right edge of the center section. Press toward the background pieces. Trim the ends of the center panel if the fabric width was less than 42½″.

7. Assemble the quilt back to measure 46″ × 46″.

8. Layer the backing, batting, and quilt top. Baste with your preferred method.

Quilt top assembly

Ready, Set, Quilt!

I suggest a neutral thread for quilting. Your quilting will really show on the background piece, so pick a pattern that you like. Take this opportunity to showcase free-motion techniques or bold straight-line quilting. An allover pattern works well on this quilt's small scale. If you really want to make the pieced block stand out, quilt that section differently than the background.

Finishing

1. Trim the excess batting and backing, square up the quilt, and attach the binding.

2. Wash the quilt and wrap it around your favorite baby.

Turn Up the Volume

Just about any color combination goes when it comes to this quilt. Bright background or neutral! Pure scrappy love for the pieced square or a controlled scheme! No matter what you decide, you can make the quilt shout it out.

Beach Grass

Finished quilt: 64″ × 90″ | **Finished block:** 8″ × 9″

Made by Cheryl Arkison, quilted by Janet Madeyski

Fat quarter friendly

There is no dreamier place than a beach. It doesn't matter whether the beach is in the Caribbean or on a prairie lake. As long as I have sand under me, water in front of me, and grass behind me, I'm in heaven. This quilt is an homage to some of my favorite beaches in Atlantic Canada. These beaches have a particularly dreamy feel when the tones of the water, sand, grass, and sky all blend together. One day I will have a little cabin that will remind me of the beach, and this quilt will live there with me.

I wanted to emphasize the vertical nature of grass in this quilt, so the blocks aren't square. If you prefer square blocks, feel free to make them square. As with most quilts that come together with a straightforward patchwork layout, the best way to change the size of this quilt is to add or subtract columns or rows of blocks.

Choosing Fabrics

I chose the colors in this quilt to reflect the marriage of sand to sea to sky. Hushed tones of blues, grays, greens, and beiges combine with pops of more saturated versions of those colors. This kind of quilt benefits from that mix of quiet with a bit of bright to keep it from falling totally flat. This quilt has many fabrics with similar values, so the mix of textures is especially important. Stripes, dots, blenders, and more add dimension, as do the hits of brighter colors.

The pattern is written to take advantage of as many fabrics as possible, but you can stick to just one or a few background choices to change the look of the finished quilt.

Note

If you have directional fabrics, you will need additional yardage of that fabric or additional fat quarters in total. You will not get the block length needed if the fabric design runs parallel to the selvage.

Materials Needed

Amounts are based on a fabric width of 42˝.

Quilt top: 30 fat quarters

Batting: 68˝ × 94˝

Backing: 5½ yards

Binding: ¾ yard

If you want the quilt backing to be made from the same fabric, you will need all 5½ yards, and you will have a nice piece left over. Otherwise, you can buy 4 yards of fabric and piece together the remainder, as needed.

Cutting Instructions

Quilt Top

To yield longer strips, cut on the crosswise grain of the fat quarters (from selvage to cut edge).

- From each of 22 fat quarters, cut 2 strips 8″ wide and, if possible, 1 strip 2″–3″ wide.

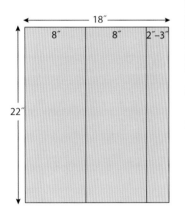

Cut fat quarters.

- From 8 fat quarters, cut additional strips 2″–3″ wide to total 44 narrow strips.

Binding

- Cut as needed for your preferred method of binding.

Some Assembly Required

Seam allowances are ¼″.

1. Cut the 8″-wide strips in half lengthwise. Don't worry about being precise; just aim to cut them roughly in half.

2. Sew a contrasting 2″–3″ strip between the 2 halves of the 8″ strip. Press the seam allowance open or toward the center strip. Figure A

3. Trim the piece from Step 2 into 2 blocks, each measuring 8½″ × 9½″. Keep the center strip in your block vertical. However, you can cut it a little bit wonky, if you like, to add variety to the placement in the quilt. Figure B

4. Repeat Steps 1–3 to make 88 blocks total. You should get 4 blocks from each fat quarter. Your finished quilt will include only 80 blocks. Making a few extra blocks isn't more work, and the added variety in blocks results in more of a scrappy look. Use the extra blocks on the back of your quilt or as the start of a baby version of *Beach Grass*. Alternatively, use 20 fat quarters to start and make 80 blocks only.

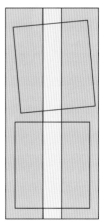

A. Sew strips together.

B. Cut blocks 8½″ × 9½″.

> "*With no ocean in sight, I settled for rainstorms and movies that take place near the ocean to keep me company while making this quilt:* The Life Aquatic with Steve Zissou *and* Finding Nemo *(for when the kids were awake)*."

5. Arrange the blocks into 10 rows of 8 blocks each. This is a fun, scrappy-looking quilt, so aim for a balance of colors, without too much of one color in any one place—but don't worry too much. If you cut your blocks wonky, you can align the angles of the center strips by row or column.

6. Assemble the quilt top using chain piecing (page 137). If you are pressing the seams to one side, be sure to alternate the directions so the seams nest when you sew together the rows.

7. Sew the rows together and press the seams open or in one direction.

8. Assemble the quilt back to measure 68˝ × 94˝.

9. Layer the backing, batting, and quilt top. Baste with your preferred method.

Ready, Set, Quilt!

For the quilting on this, I wanted to focus on the idea of beach grass blowing in the breeze. This is quite an angular quilt, so we (my longarm quilter and I) went with wavy lines. The lines come together, cross over, and go back again, much like the grass would wave in the wind. Gentle curves are a cinch with your walking foot if you gently guide the quilt through your machine. Like its inspiration, the beach grass in this quilt doesn't need much to make it move.

Finishing

Trim the excess batting and backing, square up the quilt, and attach the binding.

Turn Up the Volume

High-contrast blocks give this quilt a completely different look. Whether you go for a light background with bright or dark center strips or you mix it up, you will get a bold, funky quilt. This design also lends itself well to a mix of solid fabrics.

Button Sudoku

Finished quilt: 27″ × 27″

10″ precut square friendly

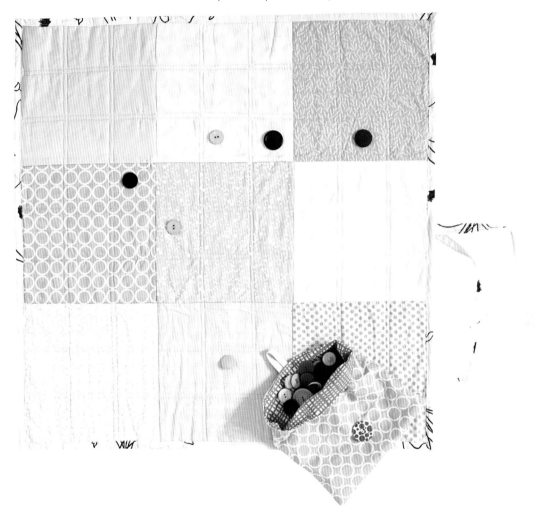

I may or may not have created a few addicts when I brought a couple of Sudoku books to a family vacation a few years back. This fun game is modeled after the famous numbers game. This one is easy enough for the preschoolers and grandparents. It travels well, pinch-hitting as a little picnic table topper when necessary.

We use buttons as the game pieces, but painted rocks also work well. Creating them is a Sunday activity itself—first the gathering of the rocks, then the painting of them.

Materials Needed

Quilt top: 9 squares 9½″ × 9½″ in the same neutral color, but with subtle variations

Button bag: 4 squares 9½″ × 9½″

Binding and ties: ⅜ yard

Batting: 31″ × 31″

Backing: 1 yard

Buttons: 82 (9 each of 9 different colors, plus 1 more of any color for the bag's button) The buttons don't have to be the same, but you do need 9 in each color.

Elastic: 4″ piece of ¼″ elastic

Some Assembly Required

Seam allowances are ¼″.

1. Arrange 9 squares into 3 rows of 3 squares each.

2. Assemble the quilt top using chain piecing (page 137).

3. Layer the backing, batting, and quilt top. Baste with your preferred method.

Ready, Set, Quilt!

Quilt the mat by stitching in the ditch between each block. Then add quilting lines at the 3″ and 6″ marks of each square. If desired, add an additional line ¼″ away from the first lines. The idea is to create a 3 × 3 grid in each block.

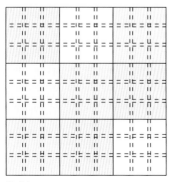

Quilting

Finishing

1. Cut 4 strips 2½″ × width of fabric.

2. To make the ties, use 1 strip to create a piece of binding tape (page 140). Fold in both ends of the strip to make a neat hem, then fold and topstitch along all the edges. Cut the strip into 2 pieces, each 12″ long from each finished end. The remaining strips will be used to bind the quilt.

3. Pin the unfinished ends of the 2 ties to the back of the quilt at the center of a side. Sew on the binding, catching the ties in the stitching. Finish binding by machine or hand.

Make the Button Bag

1. With wrong sides together, sew together 2 matching 9½˝ × 9½˝ squares on 3 sides. Repeat this step with the remaining 2 squares.

2. Clip the corners. Turn one bag right side out. Fold and press a ½˝ hem at the open end of each bag. With wrong sides together, slide one bag inside the other.

3. Make a loop with the piece of elastic. Pin it in the center of the pressed edge on one side, with the loop to the outside.

4. Align the top edges and hem ¼˝ from the edge. Make sure you catch the ends of the elastic.

5. Sew a button to the other side of the bag, 4½˝ from the bottom.

6. Fill the bag with the buttons. Fold over the top edge and slip the elastic around the button to close it.

Storing

Fold the quilt in thirds, with the ties on the outside. Place the bag on the folded quilt and roll up the quilt around the bag for transport and storage. Use the ties to hold everything together.

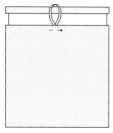

Put button bag together.

Playing the Games

Here are two different games to play with your new Button Sudoku.

COLOR SUDOKU

In the traditional Sudoku game, the goal is to have one of each number 1–9 in each row, column, and 3 × 3 grid. The same goes for Color Sudoku.

1. Set out the quilt and have the button bag handy.

2. Take turns drawing buttons and placing them on the mat: a different color per row, column, and grid. Keep drawing until no more buttons can be placed within the rules.

COLOR MATCHING

For the younger set, who might not grasp the concept of Sudoku, turn this into a color-matching game. It's another way to learn colors and spend some time with the little ones.

1. Set out the quilt with the button bag handy.

2. Take turns drawing buttons and placing them on the mat: one color only in each 3 × 3 grid.

3. The game is over when all buttons have been placed.

Parade Pennants

Finished pennant: 12″ × 10″

Fat quarter friendly

Kids love a parade. Sitting around, however, waiting for one to start, can be interminably boring. Fighting the crowds is stressful. Why not bring the parade home? Encourage the kids to pick the fabric for this project; then tromp through the forest for fallen sticks. If you throw in some penny candy, pinwheels, and toy drums, the kids can have their own homemade parade with their friends and neighbors instead.

Materials Needed

For two pennants:

Pennants: 1 fat quarter

Binding: ½ yard

Double-sided heavy-weight fusible inter-facing: 11″ × 25″ piece, such as fast2fuse

Some Assembly Required

MAKING THE TRIANGLES

1. Make a paper template for the triangle by drawing a 9½″ horizontal line on a piece of paper. Make a mark at 4¾″. Draw a line 10½″ up from that mark. Connect the top point to the ends of the 9½″-long line to create a triangle. Cut out the template.

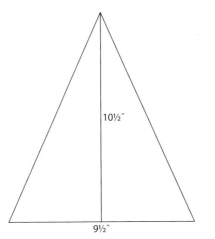

10½″

9½″

Draw triangle template.

2. Trace the template onto the fabric and the fusible and cut 4 triangles from the fabric and 2 from the fusible.

3. Make a sandwich of your fabric and fusible. Place a fabric triangle on an ironing surface, wrong side up. Top it with the triangle of fusible. Cover with another fabric triangle, right side up.

4. Following the manufacturer's directions for your fusible, press until the layers are fused together as a single unit. Repeat to make 2.

APPLYING THE BIAS TAPE

1. Cut 6 bias strips 2″ wide. Join the ends and cut a 49″ strip and a 22″ strip for each pennant. Fold and press as shown in Binding Tape (page 140).

2. To finish the ends of the bias tape, open the outer folds and press the ends under ¼″. Refold the bias tape and press again.

3. On the short side of the pennant, measure and mark 2″ from each corner.

4. Measure 8˝ from one end of a 49˝-long piece of bias tape. Pin it to a pennant at the left-hand mark. Wrap the bias tape around the triangle's edge. Make a mitered corner by folding back the bias tape on itself, leaving the 8˝ tail free and perpendicular to the edge of the pennant.

> ### Back Away from the Pins
> Use binding clips to hold the corners in place. These clips will hold better than pins, and there's no chance of being poked.

5. Sew ⅛˝ from the open edge of the bias tape, first across the end and then along the length. When you reach the pennant, backstitch for a few stitches in and out of the corner for extra reinforcement. Continue sewing, attaching the bias tape to the pennant, until you get ½˝ from the corner.

> ### Go Slowly
> Stitch slowly as you attach the bias tape. This is a fast project, but you don't need to rush through this step. You want to ensure that both sides of the bias tape are caught by the stitches. Doing this is a bit finicky, but patience will be your friend for success.

6. Fold the bias tape around the corner so that it lies smooth. Continue sewing around the pennant, folding the bias tape at the corners until you get ½˝ from the other mark. Fold the bias tape back on itself, as in Step 4, backstitching to reinforce the corner. Continue sewing to the end of the bias tape and then stitch across the end.

7. Position the 22˝ piece of bias tape by measuring 8˝ from one end and pinning the piece beside the bias tape that is already stitched on, folding the second piece of bias tape in the opposite direction.

8. Repeat Steps 5-7 to attach the bias tape to the other pennant.

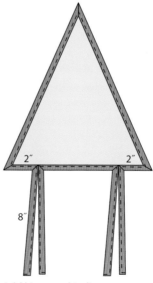

Add bias tape binding.

9. Tie the pennants to sticks, poles, or even the bedpost and let the parade begin!

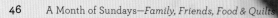

A Month of Sundays—*Family, Friends, Food & Quilts*

Eat

There is a good reason why Friday night is often pizza night for many people. Who wants to cook? It's the start of the weekend and the end of a long week. It also feels like a treat, a launch into a few days where the rules are slightly different, the bedtimes are later, and accepted laziness begins.

But there is no excuse not to eat well on the weekends. It's the time for trips to the bakery and farmers' market, mugs of coffee and hot cocoa, and good meals with good friends.

For me, it's a time to putter and experiment in the kitchen. I might make a big batch of food to take us into the coming week. Or I might try some fancy dessert just for fun. It's more about the process than the end result. Sure, we'll need to eat at some point, but I'm not necessarily in the kitchen to make dinner. Instead I'm roasting tomatoes, simmering stock, pinching dumplings, or mixing cookie dough—puttering.

Mmmm...

I love everything about cooking—starting with the search through cookbooks for recipes and dreaming about tastes. I don't even mind the repetitive prep work in the kitchen. I'm a from-scratch cook. Other than pasta and an odd box of crackers, it is hard to find much in the way of premade or processed foods in my house. Excepting chocolate, of course!

That being said, I'm not immune to burnout and exhaustion with the daily challenge of putting a good meal on the table for my family. I buy filled pasta and jarred sauce from time to time. We go out for sushi or steak when I simply have no energy or inclination to cook. Then there are the nights when we have popcorn for dinner. (If I'm feeling decadent, then it's popcorn with truffle oil and parmesan cheese and some bubbly on the side.)

My favorite moments in the kitchen, though, are the mornings. I'm still in my jammies, with the kids moving between TV and make-believe games. There is butter on the counter, always butter, waiting to be turned into pancakes, waffles, monkey bread, muffins, scones, biscuits, or maybe a fruit crisp, a cake, or some cookies. Or it might just be waiting there, soft, to be spread on bread and topped with honey.

After a snuggle with the kidlets and a consultation with my middle one, the enthusiastic baker in the family, we decide on just what the butter will be transformed into for our second breakfast. I put an apron over my jammies and tie one on my assistant. She pulls a chair into the kitchen, setting it just so, still allowing access to our tools and baking ingredients, while giving her full access to the wide counter—the perfect spot for pouring, mixing, kneading, and asking questions.

It is always her job to unwrap the butter. If she had her way, we would cook Paula Deen style—butter in everything and lots of it. She gets this from her father, a man who is still trying to get someone to make him deep-fried bacon-wrapped butter. They both settle for her unwrapping the butter and cutting it into chunks, prepped for use.

By the time the oven is warmed or the waffle iron is ready, the kitchen is a mess of flour and giggles. My young assistant is now sitting directly on the counter. It's better that way, even if her butt is pressed into an extra knob of butter, because now I have access to everything without having to navigate her chair. She's also pretty darn cute up there. From her

perch, she cracks eggs, scrapes the sides of the bowl, adds flour, and sneaks the goodies we might be popping into our baking. She also watches out the window for cheeky squirrels.

On the weekends, we actually eat breakfast together as a family at the table. There is fruit, and my husband makes his coffee instead of going out for it. Even our little girls have learned the difference between the languid eating of the weekend breakfast versus the weeknight evening meal before homework and baths. The conversations are even sillier, we don't scoff at the greater use of fingers as utensils, and maple syrup becomes a condiment for everything from bacon to tea.

It's Sunday morning.

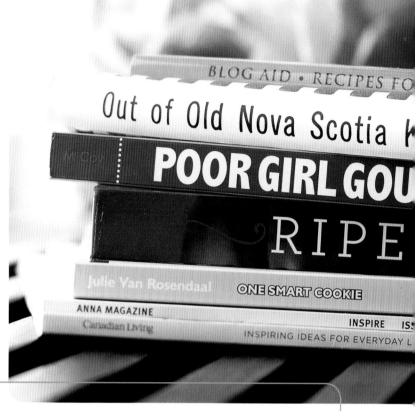

Maybe you are a weekend warrior in the kitchen, maybe not. Either way, here are some ways to enjoy the shopping, cooking, and gathering around food. Celebrate the luxury of time in the kitchen or around the dinner table. Celebrate the bounty and beauty of the food we grow and create with. Celebrate the people we share our meals with. Celebrate Sunday.

Window-Shop

When I first moved in with my husband, we had a pile of roommates. No one really used the dining room, so I turned it into my cookbook and magazine library, in addition to a place where we could actually eat. One weekend I decided to make pancakes for the whole house. One roommate grabbed her boyfriend and their coffee, settling at the dining room table. She said to her boyfriend only, "Watch this." She was referring to my habit of going through nearly every magazine in search of a recipe when I had the hankering to make something. Unfortunately for them, I knew exactly where I was going that morning. So much for their morning entertainment.

I still love browsing through my collection of magazines and cookbooks. Going online might be quicker, but I still prefer to flip pages. I pull a big stack of books or magazines to the table or the comfy chair, flip aimlessly, and chat with the family. Sometimes the girls sit with me and point out recipes they find interesting. Usually my husband just sighs because it means I'm probably spending the next few hours in the kitchen. I breathe contentment, as I get continual pleasure from these small investments.

If you do go online, any quick search with an ingredient in mind will reveal so many ideas and inspiration for Sunday dinner. Using online bulletin boards, such as Pinterest, or creating bookmarks in your web browser helps you keep track of your favorite recipe inspirations.

Gather

If you aren't a cook by nature, and you dread the hour before dinner needs to be on the table, there are still ways to find pleasure among the cutting boards and onions.

Gather friends or family to help you cook. Prepare a meal to share together or cook a big batch of something like tomato sauce, dumplings, or enchiladas. The work is easier and goes by quickly when the effort and time are shared. You can also share the effort with a potluck, with each person bringing part of the dinner.

If you don't want to cook at all, hit a local Italian market or deli. Load up on meats, cheeses, olives, peppers, and more. Add some gorgeous fruit and good wine and you have the start of a good party.

Other options include melting chocolate and serving it with cake, cookies, and fruit. Buy a great cake from a good bakery and brew some coffee. Don't worry about making it perfect or pretty. Don't feel bad if you did nothing but take it out of its box and put it on a pretty plate. Whatever you do, don't apologize for not making your dip or crackers. Just be with your friends.

Whether you cook as a group or come together over takeout, a meal shared with others is a special thing. The food serves as a backdrop to the conversation and companionship. Gathering is the important part—the food is almost irrelevant. Almost. Gather with good food and everything is just a little bit better.

When in Doubt, Bake

I must admit, I have a hard time playing dolls or cars with the kidlets. I can only fake the enthusiasm for pretend skunks and tigers for so long. When I've reached the breaking point of parenting play, I bring out my trump card—baking chocolate chip cookies. Frankly, baking anything with chocolate will divert my children from whatever they are doing into the kitchen, stools and aprons in hand before the chocolate chips are out of the cupboard.

The proliferation of brownie, cookie, and muffin mixes in the grocery stores makes me a little bit sad. Baking these things from scratch is easy and almost foolproof. If you aren't a cook or baker, then start with this easy baking. If you've kept your kids out of the kitchen until now, this is always the best way to bring them in.

Brownies, cookies, and cakes are just variations on the magic combination of butter, sugar, eggs, and flour. Change the proportions and add some other ingredients to create the individual treat. And treats they are—to bake and to eat.

Hands Off

Even if you do like to cook, there is nothing wrong with going out to eat. Especially on the weekend, when there is no real pressure to return home at any specific time. The restaurants are full of energy when you aren't. Ask your friends to join you.

In my family, we like to go out for brunch on the weekends. It is low stress for the kids in terms of behavior expectations and food choices. And it is leisurely for us parents. We can sip our caffeine, enjoy the sunshine, and not have to deal with the dishes.

It might be Friday night for Thai or Saturday afternoons at the neighborhood coffee shop. Either way, take this chance to get out, explore, and relax.

Weekend Cooking

Taken on their own, each one of these recipes is easy and tasty. Put them together for an easy weekend meal, whether that is Sunday dinner with the family or Saturday night with friends.

A GOOD SALAD

For most people, salad starts with lettuce. Frankly, that is a pretty good place to start, but it's not the only place. The possibilities are endless. Use what is in season at the market, add some nuts or a bit of cheese for an added dimension, and toss with a simple citrus vinaigrette. Just stay away from the iceberg lettuce. Seriously, walk away from it.

- 3 cups loosely packed greens (mesclun, spinach, baby greens, young beet leaves, butter lettuce, and so on—mix it up each and every time)

- 2 cups added veggies or fruit

- 1 cup nuts or ½ cup cheese

Potential Flavor Combinations

- Tomatoes, cucumbers, red onion, feta cheese, pine nuts

- Peaches, tomatoes, almonds, goat cheese

- Celery, apple, walnuts, cooked quinoa, sunflower seeds

- Oranges, roasted beets, pecans

- Asparagus, poached or boiled eggs, pine nuts, mushrooms, aged cheddar

Just like in a good quilt, aim for a balance of colors as well as flavors. Make your salad pretty *and* tasty.

Basic Citrus Vinaigrette

- 1 part lemon juice/orange juice/lime juice*

- 3 parts olive oil/grapeseed oil

- 1 tsp Dijon mustard

- 1 tbsp honey or maple syrup

- Salt and pepper

Combine everything for the vinaigrette in a jar or bottle with a tightly fitting lid. Shake and toss with your salad. Store the leftovers in the fridge for a week. Let the vinaigrette come to room temperature before using.

* To make a basic vinaigrette, use your favorite vinegar in place of the citrus juice.

ROAST CHICKENS

If you are going to go to the effort of roasting a chicken, then roast two. A few minutes of prep work, an hour in the oven, and dinner is done. By making two at once, you can either serve a large crowd or ensure that you have leftovers for lunches and another supper later in the week. It also provides extra-crispy skin for the cook to steal as the chickens rest before serving. For me, that is worth the extra bird! This is the Sunday night dinner your kids will remember well into their later years.

I strongly recommend seeking out organic and free-range chickens if possible. This bird will be naturally plump and actually flavorful. The added cost will translate into a better dinner and more meat.

- 2 roasting chickens, 3–4 pounds each
- 6 cloves garlic
- 2 sprigs fresh rosemary
- 3 tbsp olive oil
- 1 lemon
- 1 medium onion
- Salt and pepper

Preheat your oven to 425°F.

Rinse the chickens and pat them dry. Remove the neck, if still attached (reserve it for the chicken stock you are going to make later). Double-check the cavity of the bird for any innards and discard them.

Carefully slide your hand between the skin and the breast of the chicken. Working slowly, separate the skin from the meat as much as you can. Wash your hands.

Finely chop 4 cloves of garlic and the rosemary. Mix them together with 1 tbsp olive oil and a generous pinch of salt. Using your hands, rub the garlic and rosemary mixture on the breasts of the chicken, underneath the skin. Don't be shy.

Place a garlic clove and half of a lemon in the cavity of each chicken. If you have butcher's twine, tie up the legs. If you don't have it, don't worry about it. Peel the onion and slice it into large rings. Line the bottom of a 9˝ × 13˝ baking pan with the onions. Place the chickens on top. Rub the chickens with the remaining 2 tbsp olive oil and season generously with salt and pepper. Wash your hands again.

Cook the chickens, breast side down, for 30 minutes. Reduce the heat of the oven to 375°F, carefully flip over the chickens, and cook for another 30-35 minutes. Remove the chickens from the oven and let them rest 15 minutes before serving. Resist the urge to pick at the crispy skin that entire time.

SLOW-ROASTED TOMATOES

So maybe you aren't a meat eater. Or you are, but you want something stellar to sit beside your roast, potentially stealing all the attention. These tomatoes will do it. Serve them on crusty bread slathered with goat cheese and topped with fresh basil. Or toss them with pasta, some feta cheese, chopped rosemary, and a splash of balsamic vinegar. Make twice as many as you think you need, because I guarantee that half of them won't make it to the dinner table. You will be eating them like candy as soon as they come out of the oven. They are perfect weekend food, because 5 minutes of prep and 5 hours or more in the oven make for sublime eats.

- 4 lbs. Roma tomatoes
- 4 tbsp olive oil
- Salt and pepper

Preheat the oven to 300°F.

Wash then cut the tomatoes in half. Spread them out on baking sheets. They can touch one another, but you don't want them in a pile. Drizzle them with the olive oil and give the pan a little shake. Generously season with salt and pepper. Put the pan in the oven and leave them to roast for at least 4 hours. If you can be patient, try another hour or so. The tomatoes are ready when they look just a bit dry and shriveled. They will be about half their original size.

CITRUS CURD

I have a serious addiction to lemon curd. My favorite is made with Meyer lemons, when they are in season. Meyer lemons are sweeter and less tart, which makes for a very rich curd. Any citrus fruit will do, however—lemons, limes, oranges, blood oranges, even grapefruit.

Serve the curd on top of yogurt for breakfast, in a tart shell, straight with a pile of fruit, right from the bowl with a big spoon, or in a mound of cooked egg whites (a pavlova) for a fancy dessert. Our favorite way is in a bowl with a buttery, crumbly cookie for dipping.

- 3 whole eggs
- 3 egg yolks
- ¾ cup sugar
- ½ cup citrus juice
- 1 tbsp zest (*optional*)
- 3 tbsp butter

Combine the eggs, egg yolks, sugar, and citrus juice in a medium saucepan and whisk it together well. Cook on medium heat, whisking nearly constantly, until it is foamy and thickened. This should take 3–5 minutes. It might boil just a little as it thickens. Remove the mixture from the heat as soon as it thickens.

Strain the mixture through a fine sieve into a clean bowl. Add the zest, if using, and butter. Whisk until the butter is melted.

Place plastic wrap right on the surface of the curd or transfer it to a jar. Let it cool in the fridge until thickened further and chilled.

WHOLE WHEAT BROWN SUGAR SHORTBREAD WITH COCOA NIBS

I love chocolate chip cookies as much as my kids do. But every now and then, I want something a bit different. These cookies fulfill all my cookie requirements—a clear taste of butter, the richness of brown sugar, a slight crumble that falls to a mess on my lap, and any sort of cocoa goodness.

Find cocoa nibs at health food or high-end grocery stores. Roast them for a few minutes in a hot oven for an intensified flavor. If you can't find them, substitute mini chocolate chips.

Preheat the oven to 350°F. Butter or spray with nonstick spray a 9˝ round cake pan or 9˝ × 9˝ baking pan.

Whisk together the flours and salt in a medium bowl.

In a sturdy bowl, stir together the butter and brown sugar until creamy, using a big spoon or an electric mixer. Add the vanilla and mix well. Slowly add the flour to combine. Add the cocoa nibs.

Pat the mixture into your prepared pan. Bake for 20–25 minutes until lightly golden. Remove from the oven and let cool for 5 minutes. Cut the cookies into triangles (if you are using a round pan) or squares. It is important that you cut them while warm, otherwise you won't get them cut at all. Let cool completely before you enjoy them.

- 1 cup all-purpose flour
- ½ cup whole wheat flour
- ½ tsp salt
- 1 cup butter, softened
- ½ cup brown sugar
- 1 tsp vanilla
- 2 tbsp cocoa nibs

Crossword

Finished quilt: 76″ × 76″ | **Finished block:** 4½″ × 4½″

Made by Cheryl Arkison, quilted by Angela Walters

Charm pack, fat quarter, or fat eighth friendly

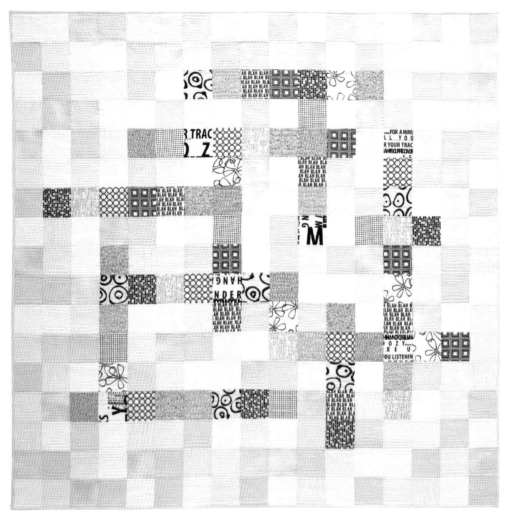

Full confession: I've never done the famous (or infamous) *New York Times* crossword, and I'm not sure I ever will. However, while on bed rest with my first baby, I made my way through books and books of crosswords to keep my brain engaged. Since then, I enjoy the bits of time I do have to work on a crossword puzzle. What better way to take advantage of that time with the newspaper and pen (yes, pen) than with a crossword puzzle–inspired quilt?

Easily change the size of the quilt by changing the size of the block or by playing with the layout. Try making up your own crossword puzzle and using that for your layout. Adjust the number of squares needed for the "words" and background as needed when doing a custom layout.

Choosing Fabrics

The key to this quilt is having contrast between the "words" of the puzzle and the background. If the black/white/gray scheme isn't to your liking, play around with colors. You can use a single fabric for the background, but mixing it up provides much more visual interest. Keep in mind that a larger variety of fabric means more variety in your squares and a good depth of variety for the background.

Always keep value in mind, so your word squares stand out from the background.

This quilt is designed with charm packs in mind, just to make it easier, as they are already in 5˝ × 5˝ squares. The material requirements provide yardage if you don't have charm squares. If you are using charm squares, the Cutting Instructions indicate how many squares are needed.

Materials Needed

Amounts are based on a fabric width of 42˝.

Word fabric: 6 fat quarters or 18 fat eighths

Background fabric: 4¾ yards total
(or 10 cuts of ½ yard each)

Batting: 81˝ × 81˝

Backing: 4¾ yards

Binding: ¾ yard

You need just slightly more than 9 pieces, so expect a bit of leftovers in your background fabric or raid your scrap bin for the extra required.

Cutting Instructions

WORD FABRIC

Cut 71 squares 5″ × 5″, the more variety the better.

BACKGROUND FABRIC

Cut 218 squares 5″ × 5″, the more variety the better.

BINDING

Cut as needed for your preferred method of binding.

||||||||||||||||||||||||||||||||||||||||||||||||||||||||||||||||||||||||||||||||||||||||||||||||||||||||||||||||||||||||||||||||||||||||||||

Some Assembly Required

Seam allowances are ¼″.

Note: The following instructions refer to the quilt as it is shown in the project photos. If you would like to create your own layout, I suggest using a design wall or flat surface and arranging your words first, before filling in the background.

1. Arrange the squares into 17 rows of 17 squares each. You can follow the assembly diagram (page 62) or arrange the squares in a way that works for you. Arrange all the blocks on a flat surface (design wall, bed, or floor).

2. Assemble the quilt top using chain piecing (page 137). If you are pressing the seams to one side, be sure to alternate the direction so the seams nest when you sew the rows together.

3. Sew the rows together and press the seams open or in one direction.

4. Assemble the quilt back to measure 81″ × 81″.

Although you can piece a quilt backing from two large strips of fabric, it is actually better to piece it in thirds. Put one full width of fabric in the middle, cut the other piece of yardage in half, and then sew the pieces to either side of the middle piece. This may be an extra step, but it will help the quilt wear better over the long run.

5. Layer the backing, batting, and quilt top. Baste with your preferred method.

Ready, Set, Quilt!

The layout of this quilt was indeed done with specific words in mind. Those letters are quilted in each designated square. It's a nice touch on what is essentially a simple quilt. After stitching the letters, an allover design fills the background to add great texture. If you prefer a simpler design, I suggest a diagonal grid or a grid that echoes the seamlines.

"*It is impossible to stitch and write at the same time. Thus, while you are sewing on the binding is a great time to share the crossword with your partner. Let your partner read the clues and wield the pen, while you stitch away.*

Now, where is the paper and my cup of tea?"

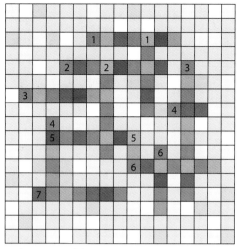

Quilt top assembly

Finishing

Trim the excess batting and backing, square up the quilt, and attach the binding.

Turn Up the Volume

With construction based on charm squares, now is the time to pull out all of your precuts. Value is very important to maintain the integrity of the design. Ensure high contrast between the words and the background. That doesn't mean you can't use bold, printed fabrics throughout the piece; just make sure you have good value contrast. Mix up your charm packs and showcase your favorite fabrics in this updated patchwork.

This pattern is based on real words making up a real crossword. Take a few minutes to fill out the crossword for yourself.

Across

1. Laughter emanating from little kids

2. Light from the sky

3. Sometimes we have to stop and do this

4. Babies do it, why can't we?

5. In the midst of it all, this gives us a break

6. Afternoon break, imported from the Brits

7. Unwind, combination of two words (slang)

Down

1. Stopping, doing nothing

2. Teenagers do it, why can't we?

3. Quilting, the ultimate in

_____

4. Not breakfast, not lunch

5. To fuel our tummies

6. One foot in front of the other, down the avenue

Find the answers on page 143!

Sherbet

Finished quilt: 78″ × 85″ | Made by Cheryl Arkison, quilted by Angela Walters

Fat quarter friendly

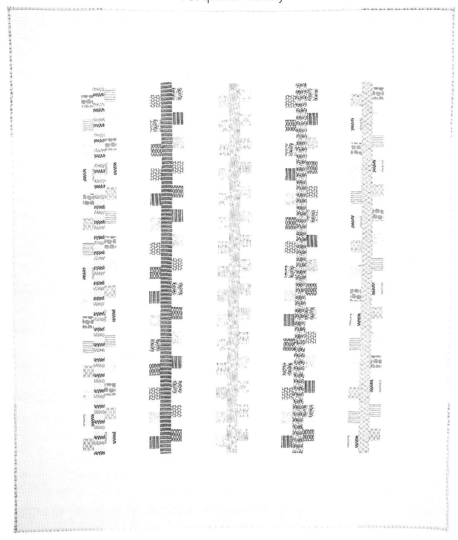

When my parents got married in the mid-1960s, their wedding colors were mint green, peach, and yellow. I was always drawn to the sunny nature of their wedding photo. Of course, that may have had something to do with the oh-so-cheerful peach and forest green combo I had going on in my room (yes, it was the 1980s). Obviously, I had those colors on the brain when designing this quilt. The orange, green, and yellow combo makes me think of sherbet, my parents' wedding, and pure, sweet summer pleasure.

To change up the size of this quilt, you can make the pieced columns shorter, use fewer or more columns, or change the size of the background columns. I do recommend sticking to an odd number of pieced columns for the best overall design, though.

Choosing Fabrics

The small scale of this quilt's confetti pieces requires careful fabric selection. To maintain the design effect, you need to steer clear of large graphic prints that have a lot of white space. Instead, stick to prints that will provide good contrast with your background choice. Scale and value are very important in this quilt.

This quilt has more background than print, with the design floating on a sea of creamy white. The color of the background is not as important as ensuring good contrast with the confetti pieces. Pick three colors that you won't be tired of looking at while piecing and quilting.

For a wilder, confetti-streamer effect, make each column multicolored.

Materials Needed

Amounts are based on a fabric width of 42˝.

Confetti pieces: 5 fat quarters each of 3 colors (for maximum variety)

Background fabric: 5¼ yards

Batting: 82˝ × 89˝

Backing: 5¼ yards

Binding: ¾ yard

Cutting Instructions

CONFETTI PIECES

To yield longer strips, cut on the crosswise grain of the fat quarters (from selvage to cut edge).

- Cut 2 strips 2½˝ from each fat quarter.

- Pick 2 fat quarters from each color range to become the center strip on the columns. Cut an additional 3 strips 2½˝ for each center strip. (If the width of the fat quarter is less than 21˝, cut 1 more strip.)

BACKGROUND FABRIC

- Cut 16 strips 2½˝ × width of fabric; from 1 strip, cut 12 squares 2½˝ × 2½˝.

- Cut 6 strips 6½˝ × width of fabric. If your fabric is less than 42˝ wide, cut an additional strip to total 7.

- Cut 7 strips 12½˝ × width of fabric. Trim just the selvage; you want to keep as much length in each strip as possible.

BINDING FABRIC

- Cut as needed for your preferred method of binding.

Some Assembly Required

Seam allowances are ¼˝.

MAKE THE CONFETTI COLUMNS

1. Using the 2½˝-wide strips, sew 2 print strips to each background strip. Press to the print strips. Make 10 sets.

Piece strips.

2. Cut the pieced strips into 2½˝ sections to make 4½˝ × 2½˝ sections. Cut 12 sections from each set.

3. Sew 15 sections from Step 2 end to end. Sew a 2½˝ × 2½˝ background square to a print square at one end, and repeat for both sides of each column.

4. Trim 1˝ from a background square at one end of each pieced column so they each measure 61½˝ long.

Take Care

If using directional fabric, keep its direction in mind as you are sewing together the blocks. The direction of the print changes from the first seam to the finished column.

5. Sew together 3 (or 4, if necessary) print strips for each column center. Trim to 61½˝ long.

Accurately Measuring Long Strips

Try this trick to accurately measure long pieces without stretching the fabric: Get the longest ruler you have. Lay your fabric horizontally on a flat surface in front of you. Line up the ruler with the left end of the fabric and along the bottom edge. Make a small mark with a pencil or fabric pen in the edge of the fabric at the end of the ruler. Pick up the ruler and move the fabric to the left. Smooth it down, but don't stretch it. Line up the end of the ruler with the mark you just made, making sure the ruler also lines up with the fabric's bottom edge. Make another mark at the end of the ruler. Pick up the ruler and move the fabric to the left. Repeat as many times as necessary to measure out the desired length. If you are left-handed, it might be easier to work from the right instead.

6. Pin a pieced row to a matching color center strip. Pin at the middle, and then at each end. Add 3–5 additional pins between the middle and the ends. Pinning at this stage ensures that you do not pull and stretch the strips as you sew. Sew with the pieced row on the top to make sure your seam allowances stay flat. Press the seam allowances open or toward the center strip. Add the other pieced row to the other side of the center strip. Note

> *Stitching between ice cream cones on a sunny day seems about perfect. Just keep the napkins handy.*

that on the left edge of each column, the row begins with a whole background square, and on the right edge, the row begins with a trimmed background square. Make 6.

Having Options

You have an extra column, giving you more options with respect to color placement when it comes to piecing together your quilt top. I suggest you piece the unused column into the back of the quilt.

MAKE THE QUILT TOP

1. Sew together the 6½˝-wide background strips end to end. Press the seams in one direction. Cut 4 strips 61½˝ long.

2. Sew together the 12½˝-wide background strips, end to end, into 1 set of 3 and 2 sets of 2. Press the seams in one direction. Cut 2 strips 61½˝ long from the set of 3. Cut 2 strips 78½˝ long from each set of 2.

3. Arrange the pieced columns and the 6½˝-wide background columns as shown in the assembly diagram (right). Pin together the first 2 columns, as in Step 6 of Confetti Columns (page 65). Sew and press the seam allowance toward the background column. Add the next column, pressing each seam as you go, until the columns are joined.

4. After all the 6½˝-wide columns are sewn together, pin and sew the 12½˝ × 61½˝ background strips to the sides. Press the seam allowances toward the background strips.

5. Pin the horizontal 12½˝ × 78½˝ background strips to the top and bottom of the quilt top. Pin in the middle first, and then pin the ends. Add additional pins as necessary to keep either piece from stretching. Sew and press toward the background strips. Press the entire top well.

6. Assemble the quilt back to measure 82˝ × 89˝.

7. Layer the backing, batting, and quilt top. Baste with your preferred method.

Ready, Set, Quilt!

This quilt has a lot of white space, providing a showcase for your quilting. You can go bold by picking a pale version of one of your sherbet colors for your thread or keep it relatively subtle by using a thread that matches the background fabric. Allover quilting designs, whether free motion or gridded, are well suited to this quilt. If you, or your longarmer, have

the skills, look for something a little more complex to fill the background space.

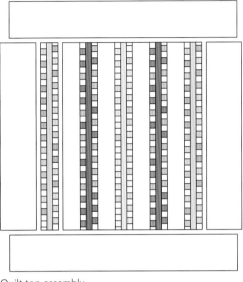

Quilt top assembly

Finishing

Trim the excess batting and backing, square up the quilt, and attach the binding.

Turn Up the Volume

Put the lighter fabrics aside and go for bold and bright on your confetti strips. Mix up the colors on each strip or try a rainbow effect. For a truly bold look, reverse the values—a dark background with light confetti pieces. Now that's the way to get the party started!

2. Use the measurements from Step 1 to draw a pattern on a large sheet of paper or directly on the wrong side of your fabric as described below. After you have the measurements, it is simply a matter of marking them appropriately and connecting the dots.

- Divide measurement A in half, and then add 2˝. Draw a line this length in the center of your pattern paper. Mark the midpoint of this line.

- Draw lines down from the ends of line A equal to measurement D. Connect the line at the bottom. It should look like a box.

- From the midpoint of line A, draw a line up equal to measurement B, minus 2˝.

- Using the top of that line, draw a line equal to line C, centered on the top of line B. Connect the ends of line C to the ends of line A.

    This is your apron shape.

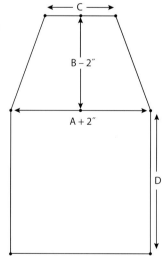

Create apron template.

3. Place and pin the 2 pieces of fabric for the apron right sides together. If you drew directly on the fabric, cut along the lines you drew. If you drew on a piece of paper, cut out the pattern on the line, place and pin the pattern to the fabric, and cut out the apron.

4. Cut the waist and neck ties from ribbon or binding tape.

Toddler: Cut 4 lengths 15˝ long.

Kid: Cut 4 lengths 19˝ long.

Adult: Cut 4 lengths 24˝ long.

5. If you are customizing your apron (see Customizing sidebar, page 72), do it now, before you sew the apron together.

6. Place the apron front on a smooth surface, right side up. At the waist, pin 2 of the ties ¼˝ in from the corner. Repeat with the neck ties. Also, pin the loose ends of the ties so that you don't accidentally catch them in a seam.

7. Carefully place the apron back piece, right side facing in, on top of the apron front and ties. Pin the pieces together.

8. Start sewing the pieces together on the apron's bottom edge. Begin sewing a few inches from one corner. Sew all the way around the edges, stopping and pivoting at the corners. Stop sewing a few inches from the other corner on the bottom edge, leaving an opening.

9. Give the seams a quick press. Clip the outside corners. Turn the apron right side out through the opening. Remove the pins holding the ties down. Turn in the seams at the bottom opening to the inside. Press all the seams.

10. Topstitch around the outer edges of the apron, making sure to catch the seams at the bottom edge.

Get in the kitchen and cook!

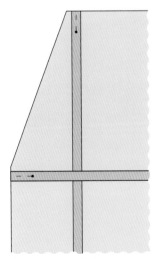

Pin ties in place before sewing.

Customizing

All of the following customizing should be done *before* you assemble the apron.

ADD A LETTER OR DESIGN

Plan the letter or motif you want to use based on the size of the apron. Select an image that you can draw or trace, perhaps a cupcake, a bird, a flower, or a spatula. If you aren't comfortable with your drawing skills, pick your favorite, noncopyrighted image from a clip-art or online source.

Draw or trace the image and refer to Easy Appliqué (page 133) to attach it to the apron. Because the apron will be washed, I suggest that you use the fusible web method and stitch around the outside edge of the shape with a satin stitch, a blanket stitch, or a straight stitch. You can do this by hand or machine.

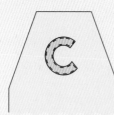
Add letter.

Add design.

ADD A POCKET

1. Make a pocket any size you'd like by starting with a rectangle that is twice as long as it is wide—5″ × 10″ for example.

2. Fold the rectangle in half, wrong sides together, to create a square. Press; then sew 2 opposite sides together. Clip the corners and turn the pocket right side out. Turn in the seams at the opening. Top stitch ¼″ from the edges.

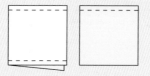
Add pocket.

3. Pin the pocket on the apron front where you would like it, perhaps on the front of the hip or on the chest. Stitch ⅛″ from the edge on the bottom and sides of the pocket. Remove the pins and press again.

Napkins with Built-In Ties

Finished napkin: 16″ × 16″

When my family gave up paper towels and napkins for the more sustainable, and frankly prettier, cloth napkin, we struggled with one small detail—we had no napkin rings in the house. Looking to limit laundry, I insisted that cloth napkins, unless filthy with tomato sauce or butter, get used for more than one meal. The only way we could then tell who used what napkin was by assigning different colors to each person. With the built-in ties and decorative edge of these napkins, I now have a coordinated set with individual markings provided by the homemade bias tape edge.

I love the relaxed look of linen for these napkins, but they will require pressing if you want a crisp look. Cotton will be similar. You can use any solid color for some gorgeously decorated tables. If you want to use a print for the napkin, make sure you like the look of the fabric on both the right and wrong sides. In a single layer, the wrong side will be quite visible. Or double up the napkin by basting two squares of fabric wrong sides together before attaching the ties and binding.

Materials Needed

Makes 4 napkins.

Linen or cotton: 1 yard

½˝-wide double-fold bias binding tape: 9¾ yards (or make your own, page 140)

Some Assembly Required

1. Cut the napkin fabric into 4 squares 16½˝ × 16½˝.

2. Cut the bias tape into 4 pieces, each 72˝ long. Cut 4 additional bias tape pieces 14˝ long.

3. Fold under the ends of each 14˝ bias strip ¼˝ and press. Topstitch across the end, along the long edge, and across the other end. These are the ties.

4. Find the center point of the 16½˝ × 16½˝ napkin square. Pin the center of the topstitched bias tape ties to the center of the napkin square. Stitch the ties to the napkin square using an X shape in a rectangle, no larger than ¾˝.

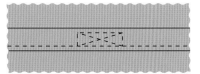

Attach tie.

5. Attach the bias tape to the edges of the napkin as if it were bias binding on a quilt (page 141). Fold the bias tape to the other side of the napkin and stitch ⅛″ from the edge of the bias tape. Use a coordinating thread.

6. Press well.

Napkin Folding

There are three easy ways to fold these napkins for decorative and functional use.

- Roll the sides of the napkin in toward the ties. When the rolled edges meet, tie the napkin closed with the built-in ties.

- Gather the napkin by pinching the fabric 2″ below the ties. Then use the ties as you would a napkin ring—tying around the gathered fabric and fanning out the edges.

- Fold the napkin in thirds, making sure the ties are on the outside. Roll the sides in and tie. This is a compact way to store or transport the napkins.

Napkin and napkin ring in one, pack them in your picnic basket or leave them on the table for brunch.

Shop

When money is no object, the object has no value. When we can buy anything we want, whenever we want, we don't value what we have. As a quilter, I could have every fabric line I desire, but then I'd have a heck of a lot of fabric languishing in piles in the closet. The value of the fabric comes in bringing it alive as I cut, combine, and create. The value is realized in a quilt, a bag, a skirt.

This means I think of my stash as a bank. It holds potential value. Really, it is like a derivative. I keep it in storage on the promise of future value. To keep my fabric house in check, I need to make sure I don't just hoard the fabric for the potential promise, but instead work to realize that promise in the here and now.

Likewise, gathering fabric just for the sake of collecting does no one any good, except the manufacturers and designers. Buy what you truly love and can afford. Don't fall victim to the must-haves your friends are hoarding. Be selective in what you spend your money on, much like you would be selective in how you spend your time on your precious weekends.

Ooh...

There was a time in my life when a stroll down the street in a busy shopping district was a fantastic way to spend a Sunday afternoon. That was when I had no kids and more disposable income. Now my Sunday afternoons are more likely to involve trips to the big-box hardware store or maybe a bike ride with the kiddos. But every now and then, I get wistful for those Sunday afternoons of old.

In those days, it was special to leave brunch hand-in-hand with my man, with no definite plans but an amble down the avenue. I married a man who adamantly hates walking, so this was the only way I could get him to stroll with me.

Our route depended on the activities of the previous night—if we needed a big, greasy breakfast, our walk was a loop through the shopping district, down the road from the café aptly named Friends and Neighbours. Hangovers in check, we would start walking. Our first stop was always the bookstore/magazine rack. In truth, this is probably the only place Hubby wanted to stop. He would pick up the latest crop of British car magazines, and I would arm myself with cooking magazines and a novel.

After that, it was the funky shoe store. Some months we could afford to actually think about buying shoes there; other months we wandered wistfully through the store, me dreaming of those awesome purple heels and he of a new pair of sneakers.

If we were still up for it at this point, I dragged him to some clothing stores to try on a million things and buy nothing more than a necklace or a T-shirt. He was patient, always. Then again, he had car magazines to read, so what difference did it make to him?

On the other hand, a low-key Saturday night meant a nice brunch filled with pastries and eggs Benedict, usually followed by browsing for furniture. We lived in the tiniest of houses, a rental that we were simply lucky to have found at the time. Furniture was a luxury of space and money. But we loved to dream.

We sat on couches, made fun of ugly lamps, and wonder about the homes we would eventually have. It was an extraordinarily good way to determine whether we would mesh well when we lived together. Would he be okay if I wanted a red room? Did I care about the construction of that couch as much as he did?

Could we both be comfortable in those dining room chairs, even though we have radically different butts?

In those afternoons, I learned that his dream home is a giant bungalow, that like all men he wanted a giant TV (but refused to have an ugly couch), and that we both love midcentury modern design. We agreed that one day we would have a house with a wraparound porch and that the best sofa would be one that is both deep and long enough for him to sleep on.

It seems silly now, ten years into homeownership and three kids later, to look back at afternoons spent furniture shopping as romantic, let alone telling of our future (especially because we still have furniture to shop for). Only now furniture shopping requires a babysitter or dividing our attention between choosing the right table and making sure our kids aren't wrecking anything in the store. But that's our life now. Come to think of it, I don't miss those lazy Sunday strolls down the avenue at all. They brought me the life I have now.

Just don't get me started on car shopping.

For many among us the idea of going to a mall on the weekend is torture. The mall does not have to be part of your weekend plans! In this age of online shopping, make a push to support small businesses. Link arms with your sweetie, hold hands with your littles, and take a stroll down Main Street.

Buy without Purpose

This is your chance to try something you've never had before. Maybe it is a new-to-you vegetable at the farmers' market, a dress you've eyed that is now on sale, or the just-released book by a trending author. Shopping on the weekend is often without purpose, so treat yourself and buy without purpose, too—well, as much as the budget allows.

Sunday Shopping

In some communities, stores are closed on Sundays. Instead of letting this drive you batty with lost opportunities, let it guide you to take a different route—grab a coffee and window-shop. Stroll down a street with interesting stores, look through the windows, and imagine all that you would buy with a million dollars. A little dreaming goes a long way.

Even if your stores are open on Sunday, window-shopping is perfect for the early-morning or late-night crowd. The streets are quiet, and the windows are the focus of attention. Now you can really see what the stores were hoping to do with their displays, instead of fighting crowds of shoppers just for a glimpse.

The act of dreaming, wishing, and plotting gets your brain working creatively. It isn't any different from flipping through home magazines or quilt books. It can be just the right poke to your creativity to get you going on something new.

Farmers' Market

Farmers' markets are perfect for exploring the communities around you, without having to leave your own. Producers come to sell their wares and their stories. Don't just pick up the flowers or the homemade pie. Pick up the story of the person selling you the treat. Knowing the people behind the food is as important as where it comes from, how it is grown, and how to cook it.

There are other families that go to two farmers' markets a week for groceries, but I think we are the exception, not the norm. If you haven't been to your local market lately, what's stopping you? Swing by to stroll through the aisles, the field, or the gravel parking lot.

The market is also great for crafts and artisan goods. If you are looking for a birthday present or unique gift, browse the booths filled with yarn, jewelry, and more. You are pretty much guaranteed something creative and unique, perfect for when you don't have the time to make a gift yourself.

Lemonade Stands

I should have a bumper sticker that states, "I Brake for Lemonade Stands!" In fact, come summer, I keep cash in my car for the express purpose of buying at any lemonade stand I should happen across.

As kids, we would often set up on the corner, with lemonade or powdered iced tea. Really, though, my friend and I were trying to sell our painted rocks; the drinks were just a side business.

If your kids are old enough and so inclined, I would definitely encourage them to try their hand at this most fundamental start to entrepreneurship. Find a relatively busy corner where you can feel comfortable that they are safe. Then help them get stocked with lemonade—preferably the real stuff—and even help them spread the word with social media. (Painted rocks are optional.)

Browse the Books

I can happily spend an hour or two walking up and down the aisles of even the smallest bookstore, pulling books and daydreaming about the time I might have to read them. But I find it nearly impossible to enter a bookstore without buying something.

Hit the sections you might not normally buy from to see what's out there—maybe a new interest will be sparked. Dig through the piles at the used bookstore for loved books for a great price. Pick up something trashy for pure pleasure.

Take your kids along, too. My favorite store in town has an adult side and a kids' side. I can be on my side and see and hear them all the time. The staff doesn't mind kids pulling things down to explore, so long as I make sure nothing is wrecked and everything gets put back. But I've trained the kidlets to return items to the shelf so as not to interrupt my browsing time. In the end, we all usually leave with a treat.

Don't forget the library too. These are free treats, provided you return your books on time.

Go It Alone

It is often on the weekend that those of us with kids will get the chance to have some alone time. Leave your partner in charge of the kids, so you can run errands or shop unencumbered.

Even if you are just heading to the grocery store, this kind of shopping feels indulgent. When you are at the store alone, you have the luxury of reading every label on every shampoo bottle so you can pick just the right one or of spending fifteen minutes in the magazine aisle. Just the peace of not having to repeatedly say "no" and keep sticky fingers off everything is enough, even when all you're buying is milk.

Alone time in a fabric store? Now that's a real luxury. Wandering, pulling, stacking, and dreaming. No impatient toe taps from a partner or spending more time putting bolts away after the kids pull them out.

Master the Simple List

As much as we want to spend Sunday afternoons in a hammock with some iced tea and a good book, it's a luxury we need to create. While we steal the moments to relax when we can, what can we do when the weekly chores get in the way? Make them as simple as possible.

Grocery shopping for the week is often a weekend activity. With various diets and special requests, just getting the groceries can amount to a full afternoon of work. You can simplify that process by creating a master grocery list to streamline your shopping and ensure that your house remains stocked, minimizing weeknight forays to the store. It also saves you money because you are focused at the store and less likely to buy something just because it's there.

Here's how to create and use a master grocery list:

1. Take stock of your pantry and standard recipe lists. Start by listing all the ingredients you use on a regular basis. Don't worry about sorting them at this point; just get them down on paper.

2. Look in your fridge for all the condiments, dairy, and produce you use weekly. Your produce may change by the season or with what's available in the market, so don't worry about that as much. But if you always have lemons for your tea and frozen blueberries for your oatmeal, write those down.

3. Next time you are at the grocery store, note the aisle numbers and what each aisle contains.

4. Now there are two ways you can sort your grocery list. You could organize your list to reflect the way your kitchen is organized: baking supplies, condiments, basic pantry items, and so on. This is a great way to do it if you have a large household where many people are either cooking or constantly coming in and out of the kitchen.

The second way to organize is by the way you walk the aisles in the grocery store. If more than one person does the shopping, this is a great way to minimize time in the store and avoid backtracking because you missed an item. Most grocery stores are organized in a similar fashion and put similar items together.

Use a table in a simple word-processing program, build a spreadsheet, or even handwrite and copy your master grocery list. Leave some empty spots for seasonal items or special requests. Use specific brand names if someone else is doing the shopping and you have a preference. Then print out multiple copies. You will use one a week, so print out at least a few months' worth. And definitely use pretty paper.

5. Post your master list in an easily accessible spot in the kitchen—the fridge, on a cupboard door, pinned to a bulletin board. Make sure there is a pen available with the list.

6. Now you need to give an orientation to everyone in your household. If you finish something, mark it on the list. If it will get finished in the coming week, mark it on the list. If you want something in particular, mark it on the list.

Before you head out the door to grab the weekly groceries, make sure you have your list, your bags, and your floral wrap (page 98)—with the money you save with this focused shopping, you can pick up some flowers as a treat.

Hugs and Kisses

Finished quilt: 90″ × 63″ | **Finished block:** 9″ × 9″

Made by Cheryl Arkison

Fat quarter and 10″ precut square friendly

You'll never find me far away from a piece of paper and pen. If my sketchbook isn't handy, I'll doodle quilt concepts on anything. My daughters love to sketch quilts too. This quilt comes entirely from a sketch my daughter made. She was learning how to play tic-tac-toe, and her random scratches of X's and O's struck me for their graphic nature. Together we drew and came up with this quilt.

To make this quilt both easy and representative of the initial inspiration, the X's and O's are raw-edge appliquéd to the background pieces. You could piece the X's precisely or in an improv style if you prefer. Hand appliqué the O's for a more refined look.

Choosing Fabrics

The color scheme for this quilt came from a store window. It was a clothing store for girls (older than my daughters, but much younger than me), so I've never been in the store. But I stopped and stared at the window forever because the combination of peach, pink, and gray was entrancing and ethereal. When I started pulling fabrics, the combinations were initially a little too soft, but the blue was the jumping-off point to some contrast.

There isn't a lot of contrast of value, however, in the fabrics within the quilt. The values blend quite a bit, softening the quilt even more than the colors do. Therefore, it's important to really pay attention to scale. Because the value changes are subtle, scale plays a big role.

Don't hesitate to stick with a single color background for the X's and O's if that is your preference.

Materials Needed

Amounts are based on a fabric width of 42˝.

Quilt top: 35 fat quarters (for maximum variety)

Batting: 94˝ × 67˝

Backing: 5½ yards

Binding: ¾ yard

Freezer paper (*optional*)

Fabric glue or lightweight fusible web (*optional*)

Cutting Instructions

QUILT TOP

- Cut 2 squares 9½˝ × 9½˝ from each fat quarter for a total of 70 squares.

X'S AND O'S

- Draw a template for the O's using a compass, 2 bowls/plates, or freehand to create an O shape no longer or wider than 8˝. The width of the "lines" that make up the O should be about 1½˝– 2˝. Cut out your template.

- Draw a template for the X's using a ruler or by eye. The X should be no longer or wider than 8˝. The width of the "lines" that make up the X should be about 1½˝– 2˝. Cut out your template.

- Refer to Easy Appliqué (page 133) to cut 18 O's and 24 X's from a variety of fabrics based on your choice of appliqué method.

BINDING

- Cut as needed for your preferred method of binding.

Some Assembly Required

Seam allowances are ¼˝.

1. Pair up the X's and O's with background squares. Use the techniques in Evaluating Value (page 15) to make sure there is contrast between the appliqué and the background.

2. Appliqué the X's and O's to the background blocks, using your preferred appliqué method.

3. Arrange the blocks into 7 rows of 10 blocks each. You can follow the quilt top assembly diagram (right) or arrange the blocks in a way that works for you. (For that matter, you can also make more or less appliqués to suit your design preference.)

4. Assemble the quilt top using chain piecing (page 137). If you are pressing the seams to one side, be sure to alternate the direction so the seams nest when you sew together the rows.

5. Sew the rows together and press the seams open or in one direction.

6. Assemble the quilt back to measure 94˝ × 67˝.

7. Layer the backing, batting, and quilt top. Baste with your preferred method.

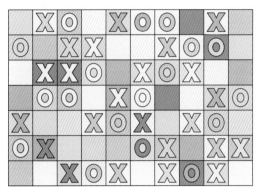

Quilt top assembly diagram

Ready, Set, Quilt!

You have choices when it comes to quilting this quilt. You can outline your X's and O's by repeating the appliqué stitching and then stitch a background design. Or you can stitch an allover design that tacks down the raw-edge appliqué. This quilt will look better the more it is used and washed, so don't fuss too much about the quilting—those raw edges will become nice and soft over time.

Finishing

Trim the excess batting and backing, square up the quilt, and attach the binding.

Turn Up the Volume

Pick your favorite color combination to give a whole pile of hugs and kisses to someone you love. A single background color with bold choices for the X's and O's is a surefire way to declare your love from the rooftops for all to hear.

> 66 *To complete the circle of this quilt, I sat with my daughter in the sun, guiding the needle as we stitched the binding down together.*"

Stripes

Finished quilt: 87″ × 92″ | Made by Cheryl Arkison, quilted by Janet Madeyski

My oldest daughter is obsessed with stripes. No, *obsessed* isn't a strong enough word to describe her love of stripes. She would tattoo herself in multicolored bands, given the freedom. Usually she just settles for stripes on all her clothes and a deep fascination with tigers. The overload of color and line is awesome, but sometimes you just need a break from all that energy. This quilt still has loads of stripes, but it is a little bit calmer, like her when she is sleeping.

The quilt is based on a mix and match of block sizes, all based on 4˝ increments. Size this quilt up or down simply by adding or removing rows and blocks. To make the quilt shorter or longer, add or remove similar-sized blocks from anywhere in each column. To make it wider or narrower, add or remove columns. For example, remove a skinny and a wide column to make the quilt twin sized or add both to make it king sized.

Choosing Fabrics

This is definitely a menswear-inspired color scheme, though none of the fabrics come from men's shirts. (They could, if you like.) The fabric amounts will ensure enough variety, minimal waste, and little in the way of repeats in the quilt.

You could also make this quilt in nearly any other color scheme. Stripes of many colors on a white background are easy to find. Mix and match to find your true stripey love.

Materials Needed

Amounts are based on a fabric width of 42˝.

Quilt top: 8 yards total (16 cuts of ½ yard each of various striped fabrics)

Batting: 91˝ × 96˝

Backing: 8 yards (pieced crosswise) *OR* 5½ yards plus fabric from your stash

Binding: ⅞ yard

Cutting Instructions

QUILT TOP

Note: Striped fabric almost always has stripes running parallel to the selvage edge on the lengthwise grain. The following cutting instructions assume you are cutting the fabric so that the stripes will all run horizontally across the quilt top. Feel free to change the direction now and then for variation.

- From each ½-yard piece, cut 1 strip 12½˝ × width of fabric and 1 strip 3½˝ × width of fabric.

- From the 12½˝-wide strips, cut:

  24 squares 12½˝ × 12½˝ (Block A)

  21 rectangles 12½˝ × 8½˝ (Block B)

  24 rectangles 12½˝ × 4½˝ (Block C)

> *The contrasting bias binding on this quilt provides some respite from the stripes. Unlike the bed-jumping frenzy the quilt inspires.*

- From the 3½″-wide strips, cut:

  25 rectangles 3½″ × 12½″ (Block D)

  15 rectangles 3½″ × 8½″ (Block E)

  10 rectangles 3½″ × 4½″ (Block F)

BINDING

- Cut as needed for your preferred method of binding.

Some Assembly Required

Seam allowances are ¼″.

1. To provide variety, this quilt consists of 3 different columns: 2 wide columns (1 and 3) and 1 narrow column (2). Arrange your blocks for the columns according to the block placement diagram. Make 3 each of Column 1 and 3; make 5 of Column 2.

If you are comfortable with improvisation, simply place the blocks in piles or bags of each size. Then grab and sew each set of columns, choosing the blocks out of the appropriate pile according to the placement diagram. Work on a single row configuration at a time to minimize confusion.

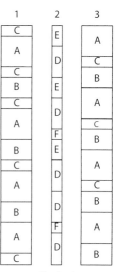

Block placement

2. Press the seams open or to one side.

3. Arrange the columns in the following order:

1-2-3-2-1-2-3-2-1-2-3

4. Pin 2 columns together. Pin at the middle and then at each end. Add 3–5 additional pins between the middle and the ends.

> ### Bring Out the Pins
>
> It might be tempting to skip pinning at this juncture. Don't. The columns should be the same length, but it is easy to stretch them as you sew. Pinning will keep things in line.

5. Sew and press the seams open or to a side. Repeat to join all the columns together.

6. Sew ⅛˝ from the outer edges to ensure that seams will not split as you handle the quilt in basting and quilting.

7. Assemble the quilt back to measure 91˝ × 96˝. This is a big quilt; therefore, the back requires a lot of fabric. The yardage requirements call for enough to piece it crosswise from a single fabric. If you have the stash, you can get away with piecing the back using 2 lengths of 2¾ yards each plus scraps pieced to make up the extra width required.

8. Layer the backing, batting, and quilt top. Baste with your preferred method.

Ready, Set, Quilt!

You can go in nearly any direction when it comes to quilting this love affair with stripes. With such a large quilt, an allover design as simple as stippling looks great. So would something more detailed, such as random spirals. Or break out the walking foot for a straight-line striped design, either echoing the direction of the stripes in the quilt top or contrasting it.

Finishing

Trim the excess batting and backing, square up the quilt, and attach the binding.

Turn Up the Volume

There is no shortage of striped quilting fabric. Turn up the volume on this quilt by picking out some of the many multicolored stripes. Don't forget about fabric that uses shapes to create stripes or that adds a curved dimension to the stripes. The combination of stripes makes this design sing.

Lush Wine Carrier

Finished carrier: 6½″ wide × 11½″ high × 6½″ deep | Made by Cheryl Arkison

When we bought our first home, location mattered the most—specifically, proximity to a grocery store, a school, and, frankly, a liquor store. My husband wanted it all to be skateboarding distance, while I wanted to be able to ride my pretty bike around. In the ten years that we've been in this house, we've made very good friends with the folks at our neighborhood wine store. But no offense to them, I think my bag for transporting libations is much prettier than theirs.

The many beautiful laminated cotton fabrics available are the perfect material for this bag. Canvas also works well, as you definitely want something heavier than regular quilting cotton. Take your time in construction, as the material is a bit different to work with. The results are worth it. Refer to the tips on working with this material on page 131.

Materials Needed

Canvas or laminated cotton: 1 yard
(or ⅞ yard and ⅛ yard for contrasting handle)

Large hand-sewing needle

Binding clips (*optional*)

Cutting Instructions

- Cut 4 panels 7˝ × 15˝ (A).

- Cut 1 panel 7˝ × 7˝ (B).

- Cut 4 pieces 12˝ × 12˝ (C).

- Cut 1 strip 2½˝ × width of fabric (D).

Cutting diagram

Some Assembly Required

Seam allowances are ½˝.

1. To make the handle, fold in the long edges ¼˝ on the long strip (D), and then fold the strip in half lengthwise, wrong sides together. Topstitch ⅛˝ from the edge on both long sides. Cut 42˝ long or try on the handle for the right length for you.

2. Mark 2 Panel A pieces at 3½˝ on the short sides and 12˝ on the long sides, as shown. Measure and mark a line from the 3½˝ mark to the 12˝ mark on the Panel A pieces.

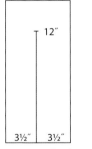

Mark handle placement.

3. Line up one end of the handle on the mark on the bottom edge. Sew the handle to the panel by sewing over or just beside the topstitching from Step 1. At the 12˝ mark, sew across the handle and down the other edge. Repeat for the other marked panel. For an added design feature, I twisted the handle a couple of times before I attached the other panels.

Attach handle.

Twist handle.

4. Sew the remaining Panel A pieces to the panels with the handles on the long side. Join all sides. You now have a square tube with a handle attached.

5. Fold over the top edge (wrong sides together) at the 12˝ mark. Topstitch ½˝ from the fold. Use a few pieces of tape to hold the folded-in fabric in place on the inside; then topstitch again near the raw edge of the folded-in fabric 2½˝ down from the top edge, removing the tape as you sew.

6. Place the bottom panel (B) right sides together to the main body of the bag, starting with just one side. Make sure the edges of the pieces line up. Secure with binder clips or pins. Start sewing ½˝ from the corner and sew from corner to corner, backstitching at the beginning and end. Line up and pin or clip the opposite side of the bottom panel with the other bottom edge. Sew and repeat on the remaining sides. *Note: If you use pins, be sure to pin inside the ½˝ seam allowance so the pin holes don't show.*

7. Sew each of the 4 C pieces into a tube. Finger-press the seams open. Without turning them right sides out, fold over the top ½˝ and topstitch to hem them. The right side of the fabric will be on the inside of the tube.

Create tubes.

8. Line up the seams of 2 tubes and hand sew down the length of the seam allowances to attach the tubes together. Repeat with the other pair of tubes.

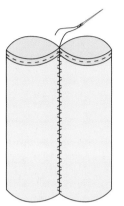

Hand stitch tubes together.

9. Stand the 4 tubes together; with some small stitches along the topstitched hemline, securely sew the pairs together.

10. Insert the 4 tubes, now stitched together, into the bag. At each corner, sew a few small stitches by hand to tack the tubes to the bag. Put the stitches into the topstitch line of the bag to hide them.

Now load up the bag with your favorite wine or sparkling water.

Floral and Herb Wraps

Finished floral wrap: 20″ × 30″ | **Finished herb wrap:** 5″ × 7½″

Made by Cheryl Arkison

You'd be hard-pressed to find a woman (and more than a few men) who doesn't love to receive flowers. In my world, a bouquet of dandelions from my kids is just as precious as a big store-bought bouquet from my husband. And when neither are forthcoming, I am not above treating myself with a bouquet. We take reusable grocery bags to the store now, so why not take reusable floral wrap? Consider it a good reason to buy yourself flowers this weekend.

Made with laminated cotton, this wrap can withstand the moisture from the flowers, and it is easy to clean. Be sure to let it dry before storing.

Materials Needed

Laminated cotton: 1½ yards (or ¾ yard each of 2 contrasting colors/patterns)

Paper: Large sheet at least 25˝ × 25˝

String: 30˝ long

Pushpin

Pencil

Binding clips

Cutting and Assembly

Seam allowances are ½˝.

MAKE THE TEMPLATE

1. Make sure your large piece of paper has a good right angle corner with straight edges. Measure 22˝ from the corner along both edges.

2. Tie the string to the pencil and measure out 22˝ from the pencil tip down the length of the string. Mark this point on the string.

3. Pin or hold the string at the 22˝ mark onto the corner of the paper. Stretch out the string the full length, use the 22˝ marks on the paper to double-check, and then move the pencil from one edge of the paper to the other to create a quarter-circle.

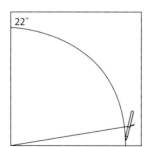
Create quarter-circle template.

4. Cut out the template.

MAKE THE WRAP

1. Square up the edges of the laminated cotton. Cut 2 squares 24˝ × 24˝. Place the quarter-circle template on the wrong side of each square. Use a few pieces of tape to hold it in place. With a fabric marker, trace the arc of the circle onto the fabric. Cut along this line.

2. Mark 2˝ from each side of the right angle corner and draw a line connecting these marks. Cut off the corners on both fabric quarter circles.

3. Cut from the remaining fabric:

1 piece 15˝ × 11˝

1 strip 2˝ × 13˝

1 strip 2˝ × 30˝

4. Fold the 15˝ × 11˝ piece in half, right sides together, so it measures 15˝ × 5½˝. Sew the long side to make a tube. Turn the tube right side out and finger-press the seam.

Use a walking foot or Teflon foot to sew the laminated cotton—it will make your life much easier.

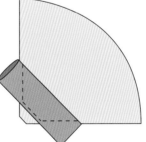

Sew and trim bottom pouch.

5. Place the rectangle from Step 4 about 1˝ up from the cut corner on the right side of the inside piece. Stitch the sides and bottom a scant ½˝ from the edge, following the side lines of the quarter-circle, not the lines of the rectangle. Cut off the excess. This creates a pouch for the flower stems.

6. Fold the 2˝ strips in half, wrong sides together, to mark a center line; then unfold. Fold the short ends in ½˝. Fold the long edges of the strip to the center line, wrong sides together, and fold in half. Topstitch all around the edges, including the ends, to make the ties.

7. On the right side of the outside quarter-circle piece, mark a spot about 11˝ from the bottom and roughly 10˝ from the right edge. Place the longer tie on the mark and stitch a box around the bottom of the tie. For extra stability, sew an X in the middle of the box. Tape the tie so that it will not get caught when the quarter-circles are sewn together.

8. Place the shorter tie on the outside quarter panel, 9˝ from the curved edge and facing the center of the panel—this end will be sewn into the seam allowance. Tape the loose end out of the way so that it will not get caught when the quarter-circles are sewn together.

9. Place the 2 wrap pieces together, right sides facing. Hold them together with binding clips. Stitch all around the edges, leaving a 6˝ opening on a straight edge for turning.

10. Turn the wrap right side out through the opening. Untape the ties. Fold in the open edge. Topstitch ¼˝ from the edges of the wrap.

Next time you head to the market, bring your wrap so your flowers will be just as pretty on the way home—with no waste.

Tie placement

Herb Wrap

Use the leftover fabric from making the floral wrap to make an herbal wrap—it's perfect for giving herbs or small bouquets from your garden.

Follow the same process as for the floral wrap, just use the following smaller sizes:

- Cut the quarter-circle template with an 8˝ radius.

- Cut the rectangle for the pouch 7˝ × 5˝, folded and stitched to make a finished rectangle 7˝ × 2˝.

- Cut the ties 8˝ and 12˝ long.

Explore

By nature, I am a risk-averse person. If I'm going to try something new, I prefer to plan it all out. In all honestly, I'd probably prefer not to try new things at all. But even I know that would make for a boring life.

Being married to a man who loves adventure and being a mother trying to raise adventurous kids means I have to stomp on the fears that make me afraid to take leaps. Because my family won't let me be wimpy, I am not. Indeed, since becoming a mother, I've become an adventurous quilter too. It is about being true to my own creativity as I try to model an honest character for my kids.

Whether it is simply about creative activities, such as quilting, or tackling an actual mountain, there are plenty of things you can do to build the skills and confidence needed to make exploration almost second nature. It is a push, indeed, but a necessary one. Otherwise those calicos will take over your life.

Whee...

I firmly believe that we are the sum of our experiences. Positive and negative, they all add up to make us the person we are at any given time. This includes the relationships we have with people and their impact on us. Date a bad boy? Subtract some self-esteem, money, and years. Cultivate a weekly date with a good friend? Add in some love, time, and laughter. We've all made mistakes and stupid decisions, we've all had good luck at times, and we've all met amazing people who change our lives. None of these things are necessarily defining of our personality or existence, but together they equal who we become.

If I hadn't met my husband, I'm pretty sure I would have a much lower number in my experience equation. The man isn't perfect, but he has indeed pushed me to be more than I ever was. In fact, that was one of his wedding vows. So far he's kept his promise.

In addition to teaching me far more about cars than I ever expected or wanted to know, my man taught me to take risks. He has a true sense of adventure. I will never be like him, but I can credit him with instilling in me a love of mountain biking, sushi, and children. He is the one who encouraged me to try surfing, flying in a helicopter, and writing a book.

Lest you think this is a one-sided relationship, let me tell you that I got him to try quilting.

My first quilt was made for our first nephew. That simple little quilt is what started my quilting addiction. As the years went by, more babies were born among family and friends. And like most new quilters, I set the goal of making quilts for all these wee babes. Every time I made the quilt and labeled it, my man insisted on putting his name on the label too. But he hadn't sewn a stitch!

Oh sure, I would make him come in the room and lend an eye to a fabric selection or maybe ask his opinion if I was playing with design options. If I was really lucky, I could get him on his hands and knees to help me baste. So long as he did something during the process, I agreed to put his name on the label.

Then came the day that my brother announced he was getting married. Without hesitation, I decided to make him and his bride a quilt. My man came along with me to the quilt shop to look for inspiration in the fabrics and the patterns. I wasn't exactly sure what I was going to make, but I knew it would be my first big quilt. A bright and bold New York Beauty quilt greeted us at the door. The door hadn't even shut behind us when my man told me that we should make this quilt.

Yeah, okay. Curves and paper piecing on what was going to be my first queen-size quilt, with only a handful of quilts behind me? Yeah, no. But as we wandered the store, we kept coming back to the quilt by the door. It wasn't just the design; it was the name too. My brother proposed in New York City—it was fate. We signed up for the class.

Yes, *we* signed up for the class. If my man was going to be a part of this gift, this complex and large gift, then he was going to sew with me.

On the day of the class, we walked into a room of women our mothers' age. I was used to this, but the ladies weren't used to seeing a twenty-something man there! They assumed he was just being a nice guy and carrying my machine for me. Then he grabbed the second machine and settled in, with our pile of fabric between us. He was his usual self—sarcastic and searching for easier ways to make the

block. Oh, and charming all the ladies in the room. Despite the fact that I was sitting next to him, more than one lady offered to set him up with her daughter.

We walked out of there with the technique down (but no phone numbers) and the start of our quilt. Over the next few months, we grabbed a couple of hours a week and sewed together. He handled the precision paper piecing for the points, and I took care of the curves. It took us forever to make that quilt, not helped by my brother often coming over unannounced in the time leading up to the wedding. But we did it, and we did it together.

My husband never quilted again.

But he did try it. I had no illusions that he would get hooked on the habit. He can sew well, but quilting isn't for him. I love him for at least trying. He went completely out of his comfort zone to explore something new.

Now, when he wants his name on a quilt, he either grabs a beer and gets on his knees to help me baste or hands me some cash and says that he bought the fabric.

Exploration is about more than climbing mountains. The push, the drive to do more and be more, is part of the adventurous spirit. That applies everywhere in our lives—from the books we choose to read, to realizing our creativity, to trying new foods. Don't be afraid; every step forward is an adventure.

Go On, Get Down

Get down with your kids or grandkids, or borrow some kids if you need to. The majority of kids have a built-in confidence when it comes to creativity. Many lose it somewhere later in elementary school, potentially becoming fearful and self-doubting adults. While they are young, however, the best thing we can do for them (and ourselves) is to get down and create with them.

My preference is to make the supplies accessible and let them lead the way. All I might do is dictate whether there is glue or paint involved, depending on my desire to clean that day. I might provide a theme or ask them to suggest one. Then we get down to it.

When I paint with my girls, for example, I tend to play with shape and color in a geometric way. They feed off of me, turning their tigers and butterflies into abstract designs, and I feed off of them, borrowing their color combinations and trying to draw animals as they do. They are so unabashedly enthusiastic about creating together and supportive of what I make that I can't help but feel great. Likewise, I want them to feel confident and inspired.

Follow the Leader

Remember that childhood game where someone got to stand in front and do all sorts of crazy moves, and you had to follow them around? When you say it that way, it seems kind of lame, but there is value in the game from a creative point of view. Playing follow the leader is a great way to create muscle memory for an activity.

After you've taken your class on invisible zippers, for example, it would be very easy to forget how to do it if you never did another one. So go home and put in a whole bunch more—make a stack of pillows for your couch. The muscle memory will be created, and you aren't likely to forget when you go to sew a dress a few months later.

I am also a firm believer in tracing. To be totally honest, I don't have great drawing skills. I don't mind, as I'm not out to be an illustrator. However, I would like to keep up with my kids and their drawing. So I trace and trace and trace. This gets me used to the idea of drawing figures and shapes. It increases my comfort in doing my own sketches. Pick some of your favorite artists, including your kids.

Do Just One Thing

Overwhelmed by all the things out there you've never done but wanted to try? Bogged down by the different directions to turn? Slow down, breathe, and pick one thing—just one thing.

This has the same effect of making a to-do list and crossing off something you've already done. It is satisfying to just make that line through an item, spurring you to tackle the next thing on the list. So, make a list of the things you want to try. It doesn't have to be a bucket list. It could be as simple as pushing yourself to use a color in a quilt that you normally shun.

Don't write something down on your list just because you think you *should* do it—make sure that what you pick excites you. But if you are avoiding it out of fear alone, then put it on the list. You will indeed tackle it, after you start with just one thing.

Monthly Challenges

Setting up a monthly challenge is a great way to push yourself. This isn't about making a quilt or a dress every month (unless that is your challenge). Rather, it is about trying something new every month. Not everything you make has to be for something. It is okay to have a pile of blocks just sitting there, evidence of your efforts to learn new techniques. Really, it's okay. Someone will put out a call for orphan blocks one day, and you can pass them on. They also jazz up quilt backs quite nicely.

Be Still

As great as it is to throw ourselves to the world with energy and aplomb, there are times when just stopping can be better for our creative explorations. The world is noisy, chaotic, and brash. Some can find inspiration and thrive with their creativity in that environment, but most of us cannot.

Stillness is about more than not watching TV while sewing. Stillness comes from the moments we quiet our surroundings and mind.

In being still we are receptive to new ideas and concepts, and able to face old ones with energy.

Whether it be meditation, staring at the clouds, or mindless hand stitching, take the moments to be still, reflective, and open to the beauty. Not only will this allow us to see the pattern on the butterfly's wings as it flutters by, it will also leave us open to the pure inspiration around us.

Go on Record

One of the best ways to stick to a goal is to state it publicly. Whether you want to lose 25 pounds, finally figure out how to sew in a zipper, or literally take a hike, declaring it to friends, family, or the entire Internet is the best way to stick to your goal.

You don't have to have a blog or Twitter account to do this. Tell your partner, your daughter, your dad. Ask them to keep tabs on you, even if it makes you uncomfortable. That's precisely the point. You will do the work because you are being held accountable. This works both ways. Hopefully you are putting the effort in so someone isn't breathing down your neck. You should also have your own cheering section. Pick a venue or person who will give you the right kind of support.

Hike with Purpose

Just as it is often easier to sew when you have a specific end product or recipient in mind, it can be easier to head out on an adventure when you have a destination in mind. Aim high, climbing skyward in the mountains for a view. Or pick your daily walk to end with a stop in a calm spot for meditation.

We recently discovered Geocaching. Using GPS coordinates, you seek out spots—both urban and wild—where little caches are hidden. Sign the logbook and swap out an item that you have brought for one from the cache. A teeny tiny quilt block, perhaps? Geocaching is a great way to hike with a purpose.

Capturing Inspiration

The world is filled with beautiful images—more than we can actually see. That's because most of us don't really open our eyes to the beauty in the small, the detailed, the mundane. We look for vistas instead of looking at the crack in the sidewalk at our feet. But that crack could be artful and possibly sprouting some chamomile. And maybe that makes you think of your grandmother drying flowers for tea in a prairie home. Then you are transported to sticky afternoons in her kitchen and hanging laundry by the poppies in bloom. Alas, I digress.

That's the point, actually. When you look up, down, and around, you can see infinite examples of beauty and inspiration. Sometimes these images do nothing but inspire a memory or a smile—definitely good things. For people who create, whether it is with fabric, words, or color, this inspiration can be overwhelming.

The best way to keep that inspiration in check is to capture it. You can't rely solely on your brain to be a virtual inspiration board. Some form of documentation is required to access that memory. My two favorite ways to do that are with a camera and a sketchbook.

I am not a person who always carries around a camera—often, but not always. I do, however, almost always have my cell phone with me. It isn't a terribly fancy phone, and the camera on it isn't that great. But taking a snapshot of the detail or image in question is enough for me. It isn't about winning a photography contest; the goal is to take a moment to capture the bit that makes me catch my breath or gets me thinking of a quilt design. Then I can send the image to my email or just keep it on the phone for reference.

For those folks with fancier phones or who like to carry a camera, you can get all pretty with these images—adding filters, editing on the fly, and posting to websites instantly. That's part of the creative process too.

A sketchbook is also essential for me to capture the image. In a previous career, I spent a lot of time in boring hotel conference rooms. If you were to look at the notebooks I kept for my job, you would see they are filled with doodles and jammed with hotel stationery covered in sketches of quilts. The work itself was not always inspiring, but sometimes the room details were. Now that I no longer have that job and my time in hotel ballrooms is usually reserved for weddings, I keep a sketchbook with me.

Having all my ideas in one place also helps me stay organized. I hate looking for a little sketch, only to have it accidentally recycled because it was on a random bit of paper. The sketchbook is used for notes at classes, working out pattern details, doodling, capturing details of a light. If I pull an image from a magazine or the newspaper, I try to glue it directly into my sketchbook to keep everything in one place.

My sketchbook also serves as a bit of a yearbook or journal of inspiration. Make sure to date your sketches and even jot down where you were when you made the sketch. Tag it with what made that image, that moment, inspirational. This will also help you access your memory when going to create.

Capturing the inspiration is part of the creative exploration. It isn't necessarily a beginning, nor is it the end. Consider it the defining of a moment, but not of a project.

Pinwheel

Finished quilt: 77″ × 77″ | **Finished block:** 5½″ × 5½″

Made by Cheryl Arkison, quilted by Angela Walters

Fat quarter friendly

This quilt is purely about playing with color and scale of design. I took the basic pinwheel design and made it big, very big. There are pinwheels among pinwheels here. It makes me think of a pile of kids racing around with their faces to the wind, pinwheels a blur.

Scale the quilt up or down by altering the block size. Your finished block size will be approximately 1˝ smaller than your starting square size, taking into account seam allowances and trimming of the half-square triangles. You don't want to remove blocks because then the design will lose its impact. Keep in mind that if you go larger, you will need to piece the triangles for the large background spaces.

Choosing Fabric

Even though this is a two-color quilt, it is anything but simple. Variations in texture, saturation, and even value have your eye moving all around the quilt. Even on a restful quilt, this is important.

If you go the single-color route, don't worry about your greens (or whatever color you choose) matching up perfectly. They don't have to all be the same shade. The interest lies in the differences, not the similarities. You can certainly use only one fabric for the pinwheel blocks, but a variety of fabrics works really well. In both cases, expect some leftover strips of fabric.

Materials Needed

Amounts are based on a fabric width of 42˝.

Pinwheel fabric: ¼ yard or fat quarter each of 7–9 prints to total 1¾–2¼ yards

Background fabric: 4 yards

Batting: 81˝ × 81˝

Backing: 4¾ yards

Binding: ¾ yard

Cutting Instructions

Note: Handle cut triangles with care so you don't pull or stretch the bias edges.

PINWHEEL FABRIC

- Cut 42 squares 6½″ × 6½″.

- Cut 8 squares 6⅜″ × 6⅜″; subcut once diagonally to make single half-square triangles.

BACKGROUND FABRIC

- Cut 42 squares 6½″ × 6½″.

- Cut 6 squares 6⅜″ × 6⅜″; subcut once diagonally to make half-square triangles.

- Cut 2 squares 39⅜″ × 39⅜″; subcut once diagonally to make half-square triangles. (See Cutting Really Big Squares and Half-Square Triangles at the right.)

BINDING

- Cut as needed for your preferred method of binding.

Cutting Really Big Squares and Half-Square Triangles

1. Open the folded fabric, press, and place it horizontally on the largest cutting mat you have on a large surface like a table. Line up your ruler with the left edge of the fabric and the bottom.

2. Using the longest ruler you have, make a small mark with a pencil or fabric pen at the edge of the fabric at the end of the ruler.

3. Pick up the ruler and line up the end of the ruler with the mark you just made, making sure the ruler also lines up with the bottom edge of the fabric. Make another mark at the end of the ruler. Repeat as many times as necessary to measure out the desired length. If you are left-handed, it might be easier to work from the right instead.

4. Cut the fabric to the needed length; then fold that side up on a 45° angle. Cut off the excess fabric from the yardage piece. Press the fold.

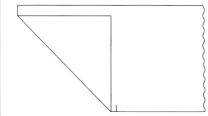

Cutting for large square

5. Unfold the fabric and use the line created by pressing to cut the large square in half on the diagonal.

> *It is best to finish the binding out of the wind, although a finished quilt is heavy enough to keep the breezes at bay."*

Some Assembly Required

Seam allowances are ¼".

1. On the back of the 6½" background squares, draw a diagonal line, using a light pencil or washable fabric marker.

2. Pair 42 print squares with 42 background squares. Sew ¼" away from both sides of the line. These are easy to chain piece by sewing the seam on one side first, and then sewing the second seam.

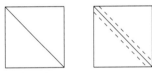

Mark and sew.

3. Cut the squares in half on the drawn line. Press the blocks flat; then press the seams toward the print fabric.

Cut and press.

4. Line up the 45° line on a ruler with the seam. Square up the blocks into 6" × 6" blocks.

5. Piece together the pinwheel units, sewing the units into columns and adding the appropriate single triangle to the end of each column as shown in the assembly diagram. Press the seams toward the print fabric.

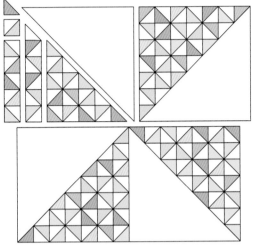

Quilt top assembly diagram

6. Sew the columns together. Press these seams open to reduce bulk. Repeat this step for the 4 pinwheel units.

7. Pin each pinwheel unit from Step 6 to a large background triangle along the diagonal seam. Take care not to stretch the fabric. Sew. Press the seam toward the background fabric.

8. Square up the entire block, being careful not to trim too much off the pinwheel blocks.

9. Refer to the assembly diagram (page 117) and sew 2 quadrants together. Press the seam toward the background fabric. Repeat with the other pair. Sew the 2 units together to complete the quilt top. Press the seam open.

10. Assemble the quilt back to measure 81″ × 81″. Put a full width of fabric in the middle and cut the other piece of yardage in half lengthwise; sew the pieces to either side of the middle piece. This avoids having a seam directly down the middle of the quilt (you already have that on the front), and it will help the quilt wear better over the long run.

11. Layer the backing, batting, and quilt top. Baste with your preferred method.

Ready, Set, Quilt!

Such large expanses of background fabric beg for some fun quilting. Try echoing the movement of a pinwheel by starting your quilting design from the center out. Either curved lines or straight lines would work well to translate the concept of a pinwheel blowing in the wind.

Finishing

Trim the excess batting and backing, square up the quilt, and attach the binding.

Turn Up the Volume

There are a lot of color possibilities to make this quilt louder.

• Use one large-scale print for the pinwheel blocks and another fabric for the background. This showcases the print in a new way and lets the design sing without falling flat.

• Use your country's colors for the pinwheel blocks to make a great patriotic quilt.

• Reverse the design—pick a bold color or print for the background fabric and a light or solid for the pinwheel blocks.

Flags

Finished quilt: *42″ × 54″* | **Finished block:** *6″ × 6″*

Made by Cheryl Arkison

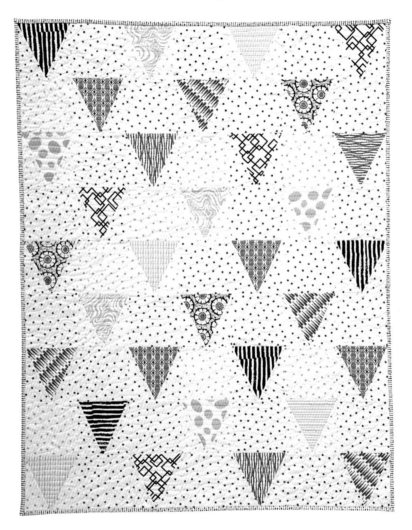

Despite my best efforts to squirrel away property by the ocean, I live in the landlocked prairies. I did live for four years in Nova Scotia, however, and there isn't a day that goes by when I don't dream about foghorns, waves crashing, and sailboats floating by. Thankfully there is a large lake nearby with a sailing club, so I can still see the boats. This sweet baby quilt is a simple homage to the maritime signal flags that always lead me back to my second home.

The quilt uses a very simple paper-pieced block. Change up the look of the quilt by adding additional background pieces or making all the blocks from flags. Easily size up this quilt by adding rows and columns or even changing the size of the blocks. When you have such a simple design, you can turn it into many things.

Choosing Fabrics

With the obvious colors of my inspiration—red, yellow, and blue—I had a lot of fun picking fabric. The background choice became very easy when I found those precious stars. I was lucky, but don't feel like your backgrounds have to match that much; a solid white would work just as well.

For the flags themselves, I sought out an array of textures: stripes in different scales, small and large patterns, and not perfectly matching colors. It adds up to a striking selection. Use one fabric in each color or mix up the fabrics used. This quilt certainly benefits from the use of four fabrics per color, even though one could have done the job.

Materials Needed

Amounts are based on a fabric width of 42″.

Flags: 1¼ yards total in 3 colors

Background fabric: 2¾ yards total in 3 colors

Batting: 46″ × 58″

Backing: 2¾ yards (pieced crosswise)

Binding: ½ yard

Freezer paper

> *Watch the Direction!*
>
> Using very directional fabrics for the background, like stripes or checks, will result in a very different effect. If you like your directional fabrics to stay on course, then stick with smaller all-over prints or solids for the background fabric choice.

Cutting Instructions

FLAGS
- Cut 32 squares 7″ × 7″ for the flag triangles.
  - 10 red
  - 12 blue
  - 10 yellow

BACKGROUND
- Cut 64 rectangles 4″ × 7½″ for the flag backgrounds, 2 for each flag.
- Cut 31 squares 6½″ × 6½″ for the alternating blocks.
  - 12 red
  - 11 blue
  - 8 yellow

BINDING
- Cut as needed for your preferred method of binding.

Some Assembly Required

Seam allowances are ¼˝.

MAKE THE FLAG BLOCKS

1. Refer to Paper Piecing (page 134) to make 32 flag blocks using the flag block paper-piecing pattern (page 122). When you make your freezer-paper patterns, make sure they are exactly 6˝ × 6˝.

2. Trim the pieced blocks ¼˝ away from the edge of the pattern piece.

3. Arrange the blocks into 9 rows of 7 blocks each. You can follow the quilt top assembly diagram (right) or arrange the blocks in a way that works for you.

4. Assemble the quilt top using chain piecing (page 137). If you are pressing the seams to one side, be sure to alternate the direction so the seams nest when you sew together the rows.

5. Sew the rows together and press the seams open or in one direction.

6. Assemble the quilt back to measure 46˝ × 58˝.

7. Layer the backing, batting, and quilt top. Baste your quilt using your preferred method.

Ready, Set, Quilt!

I chose to quilt wavy lines to bring out the idea of wind and sailing. You could also go the opposite route and quilt it with straight-line quilting to emphasize the design's linear nature. For thread, I chose to use white everywhere. There is enough white in the triangles that it doesn't matter if you don't match the thread perfectly.

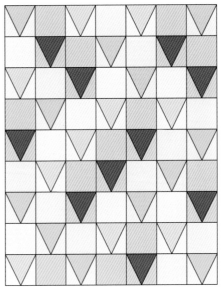

Quilt top assembly diagram

Finishing

Trim the excess batting and backing, square up the quilt, and attach the binding.

Turn Up the Volume

This design lends itself to great volume. Showcase some favorite fabrics in the flags. For extra oomph, piece the triangles themselves from scraps or strips. You could also mix up your background fabrics.

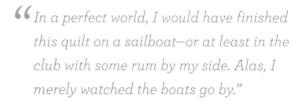

"In a perfect world, I would have finished this quilt on a sailboat—or at least in the club with some rum by my side. Alas, I merely watched the boats go by."

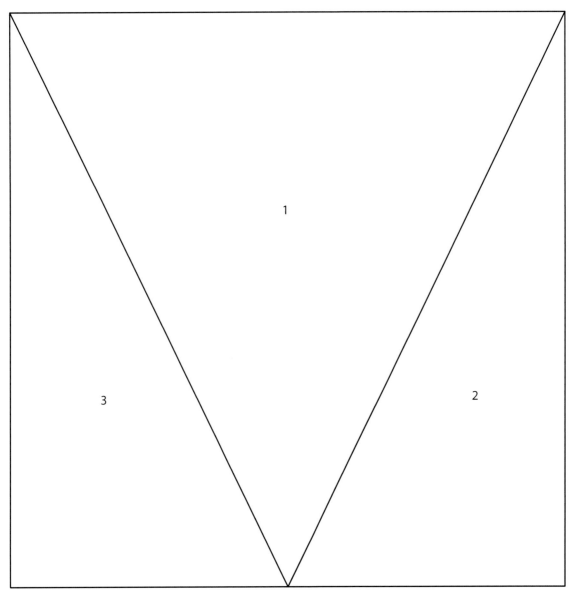

Flag block paper-piecing pattern

Treasure Bag

Finished bag (excluding handle): 14½″ × 14½″

Our family loves to stomp through the forest. Not true daylong hikes that require special shoes and backpacks, but something between that and leisurely strolls on the bike path. Inevitably I end up carrying rocks, pinecones, pretty leaves, and wildflower bouquets that the kids gather as we walk. I made these bags for the kids so they could carry their own stuff—brought and collected—on our dappled stomps in the woods.

The tie allows this bag to be flexible in length, making it adjustable for different kids and different ways to wear it. It can be carried in hand with a shorter handle, over one shoulder, or across the chest—the best carrying technique in the forest. It is also fully reversible.

Materials Needed

Bag: 1 yard each of 2 cotton or canvas/home decor fabrics

Pockets: 1 piece 12″ × 6″ and 1 piece 18″ × 6″

Paper: 17″ × 40″

Some Assembly Required

Seam allowances are ½″ unless otherwise noted.

MAKE THE PATTERN

1. Make the pattern on a large sheet of paper: Draw a 15″ × 15″ square. Make a mark in the center of the top edge (7½″ from a corner). From this point, draw a line 24″ up. Now fold the paper in half, using this line as a guide.

2. Draw a gradual curve from one top corner of the square to the top point you marked. You want the handle to be no narrower than 3″.

3. Cut out the pattern and unfold it.

4. Unfold and press the creases from your fabric. Fold the fabric in half, perpendicular to the selvages. Pin the pattern you made to the fabric. Cut out the bag. Repeat with the other fabric.

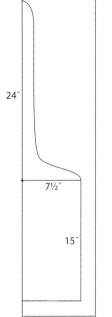

24″

7½″

15″

Treasure bag pattern shape

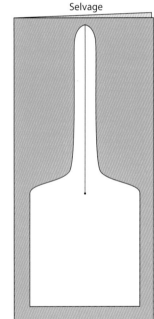

Selvage

Place pattern on fabric.

Multiply the Look by Multiplying the Fabric

If you want to have each side of the bag different and have the interior and exterior different, cut four different pieces of fabric.

5. To make the pockets, fold the scraps of fabric right sides together to measure 6˝ × 6˝ and 9˝ × 6˝. Sew around the edges, leaving a 3˝ opening. Press and clip the corners. Turn the pockets right side out and fold in the seams at the openings. Press again.

6. Pin the pockets to the bag fabrics—one pocket is intended for the exterior and one for the interior. Pin the pockets on the bag portion of the fabric where it suits your fancy, making sure that the side with the opening is either on a side or on the bottom. Don't worry too much about location; just keep the pockets at least 2˝ from any edge. Topstitch ⅛˝ from the side and bottom edges to attach it to the bag fabric. This will also sew down the opening that was used for turning. Add a second line of stitching ⅛˝ from the first one for decoration and durability.

7. With right sides facing, sew the bag portion of the exterior panels together. Press, clip the corners, and turn right side out. Repeat this step with the interior portion of the bag, but do not turn it right side out.

8. Fold and press a ⅜˝–½˝ hem on the bag handle and top areas of the bag for both the interior and exterior pieces.

9. Place the interior of the bag inside the exterior with wrong sides together. Pin and sew together by topstitching the top and handle areas ¼˝ from the edges. If desired, add a second line of stitching for decoration and durability.

Go for a hike and fill with all sorts of treasures.

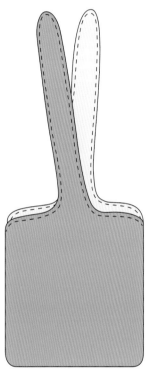

Topstitch bag and handle.

Women's Auxiliary Scarf

||||||||||||||||||||||||||||||||||||||||||||||||||||||||||||||||||||||||||||||||||||||||||||||||||||||||||||||||

Finished scarf: 16″ × 57″

Many years ago, my husband was gifted his grandfather's silk scarf from his World War II Royal Canadian Air Force uniform. My husband treasures such a personal gift from a man he greatly admired. But when Grandpa found out he treasured it so much and wasn't wearing it, boy did my husband hear about it! I've much admired the relationship they had, as well as the scarf and its history for our family. Grandpa was an adventurous soul, as was Grandma. Together, I can only hope my husband and I grow old together like they did, in love and always wanting to explore.

Because of their silky nature, voiles can be a bit tricky to work with. Cutting them out requires patience, gentle pinning, and maybe even some starch. They do sew together beautifully, however, and the effort is worth it for the drape and softness you get from voile. Refer to the tips on working with this material on page 132.

If you prefer a much longer scarf, add another ½-yard cut of fabric so that you have four sections on each side.

<u>Voile or cotton lawn:</u> ½ yard each of 3 pieces

Some Assembly Required

Seam allowances are ¼˝.

1. Cut each ½-yard piece of fabric in half on the fold, essentially creating 6 fat quarters. Trim each piece to 16½˝ × 22½˝, squaring it up as you do so. Voiles are usually a bit wider than conventional quilting cottons, so this length is easy to get. Cut them longer if you can.

2. Press each piece. Create pleats across the 16½˝ width of the fabric. Start 4˝–6˝ from one end and make a ½˝ pleat in the fabric. Repeat 2 more times to create 3 pleats. Press.

3. Make the pleats on all 6 of the pieces of fabric. It does not matter exactly where on the fabric you place the pleats; you just need to ensure that you end up with the same amount of pleating on each piece. Tack down the pleats on each side by stitching ⅛˝ from the edge of the fabric.

Make 3 pleats across width of each piece of fabric.

4. Sew together 3 pieces, end to end, on the 16½˝ sides. Repeat with the remaining 3 pieces. Press the seams open.

5. Place the 2 pieced sets right sides together and sew around the edges, leaving a 6˝ opening. It doesn't matter where the opening is, as long as it is away from a corner. Press.

6. Clip the corners. Turn the scarf right side out by pulling it through the opening. Press well to get the edges flat.

7. Topstitch a scant ¼˝ from the edges to close the opening and stabilize the edges.

> *Walk Carefully*
> Use a walking foot to stitch the voile. This foot will reduce the chance for slipping, particularly when you are top-stitching.

8. Topstitch 8–16 lines down the length of the scarf. Space them no more than 2˝ apart. Try grouping them for a more interesting look.

"*This long scarf is perfect for wrapping around you to bring warmth and beauty to your adventurous soul.*"

Basics Plus

If you are coming to an exploration of low-volume fabrics, you are likely already familiar with the basics of putting together a project. Rather than go into detail about sewing and quilting basics, this chapter covers techniques and details used in this book that are not always covered in the "basics" section of most books.

If you are a beginning quilter, do not fear—the projects in this book are not difficult. If you need some help (or a refresher), Need More Information? (page 142) includes a number of books with quilt-making basics. After you get the basics down, you can use this Basics Plus section to step up your skills and tackle all the projects in this book.

Piecing

- All seam allowances are ¼˝, unless otherwise noted.

- All seams should be pressed with a hot iron after sewing. Pressing directions are included in each project.

- A needle size of 80/12 (either a Universal or a Sharp) is recommended for all piecing.

Fabric Selection

My world is the quilting world. That means my default fabric selection is always quilting cottons. These medium-weight fabrics provide enough stability for quilts and many sewing projects, but are lightweight enough to have some drape. Different projects, however, call for different fabrics. Following is an overview of the different types of commercially available fabrics used in this book.

QUILTING COTTONS

Widely available at quilt stores, general fabric stores, and online, the largest selection of print choices is available in quilting cottons. It goes without saying that quilts are the number one use for these cottons, but don't be afraid to use quilting cottons in bags, clothes, or toys.

Fabric manufacturers use a variety of base fabrics, so not all cottons are equal. Some have more drape, while others will fray more. Large box stores that sell fabric are likely to sell a lower-quality or looser-weave cotton, even if the printed pattern looks the same. Stick with reputable stores when purchasing, and you can be assured of the quality of your cotton.

Cotton bed sheets are often of a tighter weave, particularly the newer, high-thread-count sheets. There is nothing wrong with using cotton sheets, just keep in mind that newer sheets may be more difficult to quilt. Vintage cotton sheets are often a popular choice for quilters, as the weave is looser and these sheets are often softer with their history.

LAMINATED COTTONS

Imagine a stiffer, nearly waterproof version of your favorite quilting cotton and you've got laminated cotton. Indeed, laminated cottons start with a base cloth of the quilted cotton and are coated on one side with a polyurethane film.

Laminated cottons are perfect for bags, rainwear, and table linens (wipeable!). They have limited drape to them and are relatively easy to work with. Don't use pins with them, however, as the holes won't come out in the wash. Instead, use binder clips and patience.

Oilcloth is sometimes used interchangeably with laminated cottons, but it isn't the same. Traditionally, oilcloth was a base cloth coated with a linseed oil preparation. Modern oilcloths are PVC-coated woven cloth.

> ### Tips for Working with Laminates
> In addition to skipping the pins when using laminated cottons, I recommend using a larger needle, such as 90/14. Also, use a walking foot or a Teflon foot when sewing to help your fabric move through the machine more easily.

HOME DECOR

Heavyweight and sturdy, home decor–weight fabric provides a sturdier option when making bags or items to be used outdoors. It wears well; hence its use on upholstery and drapery.

I don't recommend using home decor–weight fabric for quilting. The weight might feel nice on a finished utilitarian quilt, but it is difficult to work with. The seam allowances are thick, and it is difficult to quilt. It's possible to use it, of course, but it isn't necessarily easy.

Canvas is a good stand-in for many projects calling for home decor–weight fabrics.

VOILE

Falling on the opposite side of the weight spectrum from home decor fabrics are voiles. These are indeed cottons, but they have a wonderfully silky feel and soft drape. Traditionally, voiles were used for clothing or drapery. The proliferation of beautiful voiles from modern fabric designers, however, means they are now used in quilts to great effect.

Because of their silky nature, voiles are a bit tricky to work with. Cutting them out requires patience, gentle pinning, and maybe even some starch. They do sew together beautifully, so the effort is worth it for the drape and softness.

Cotton lawn is a similar style of fabric to voile, and these two can be used interchangeably in a project.

Use a Smaller Needle

When piecing with voile, use a smaller needle that makes a smaller hole in the fabric, either an 80/12 or a 75/11 Microtex Sharp needle, and a lighter weight thread, such as a 50-weight.

LINEN

Even though they come from different plants—linen from flax and cotton from cotton plants—these two fabrics work well together.

Linen does shrink (please prewash in hot water to avoid headaches later), and it does wrinkle. But a hot iron takes out the wrinkles. And the more it is used and washed, the softer linen gets, which makes it wonderful for quilt projects.

Like voile, linen is slippery when you are cutting and sewing. Spray starch helps alleviate any stress caused by slippage.

Easy Appliqué

About the easiest way to put two pieces of fabric together is to place one on top of the other and sew it down. I'm talking about raw edge appliqué. The look isn't for everyone—the edges of the appliqués remain unfinished, so they will fray lightly as the quilt gets loved and washed. If you absolutely hate this look, try traditional needle-turn appliqué or use a satin stitch (a very tight zigzag stitch) to stitch down the edges of the appliqué.

PREP THE BACKGROUND

Prep the background by cutting it to size. Don't forget about the seam allowances for sewing the appliquéd block into the quilt.

Find the center by folding the background block in half horizontally and then in half vertically. Finger press lightly. The lines cross at the center point. After you've appliquéd the design, you can press again to remove these marks.

Give Your Shoulders a Break

Unless you are adamant about using a single piece of fabric for the background of the entire quilt, I recommend making your appliqué background a quilt block. This way, the size is more manageable as you move the background piece while sewing down your appliqué.

PREP THE APPLIQUÉ

While you could pin the heck out of your appliqué, this is an invitation to bleed all over your block. I suggest that you use one of the following two methods to prep appliqués.

Using Freezer Paper and Glue

One of the best parts of the freezer-paper method is that there is no need to reverse the appliqué design, as long as you use the template on the right side of the fabric.

1. Draw or trace the appliqué shape directly onto the *paper* side of the freezer paper.

2. Cut out the shape on the line.

3. Press the *shiny* side of the freezer paper to the *right* side of your fabric. Use a hot but dry iron.

4. Cut out the appliqué shape. Freezer-paper templates can be used at least a dozen times before they won't stick to the fabric with pressing.

5. Use a gluestick to hold the appliqué in place with a few pins for reinforcement.

Raid the Craft Cabinet

You can purchase fabric-specific glues. But if you use a light hand with a regular gluestick, you'll be fine. After you wash the quilt, you won't even know the glue was there at all.

Using Paper-Backed Fusible Web

Using a lightweight paper-backed fusible web provides the most stability for appliqué, but it will be a stiffer block in the end.

1. Reverse the appliqué design and draw it on the *paper* side of the fusible web.

2. Cut out the design, with a ¼″ margin all around.

3. Following the manufacturer's instructions, iron the cut-out shape to the *wrong* side of your fabric.

4. Cut out the shape on the drawn line, peel off the paper backing, and place the cut-out shape in place. Iron to fuse, following the manufacturer's instructions. Discard trimmings.

> ### Go Small to Stay Soft
> For a less stiff appliqué, cut out small pieces of fusible and attach these to your appliqué close to the center and any points. This results in a more lightweight finished block.

TOPSTITCH

After the appliqué shape is on the background, topstitch it in place. Sew close to the edge, but not right on it. Or, if you prefer, you can satin stitch around the edges.

Stitch appliqué shape.

When you do the quilting, you can echo the appliqué shape, stitch right over the topstitching, or quilt an allover design.

Paper Piecing

There is something about paper piecing that instills fear in many a quilter. To be honest, I'm not sure why. Paper piecing is the easiest way to get precision in your piecing. Plus, you can see what you're doing before you sew, minimizing the potential for mistakes.

The quilt in this book that uses paper piecing (*Flags*, page 118) is a fantastic introduction to paper piecing, with just two seams. Master this easy block and you will be on your way to infinite paper piecing possibilities!

One of the most common complaints about paper piecing is that it produces a lot of waste. Or, if you work really hard to minimize waste, you increase the chance of mistakes. The best way to deal with this is to not worry about it. Cut your pieces large enough and, as you trim, see if they will work in a similar place on the next block. If not, place those pieces into a scrap bin for another project. Changing your mind-set regarding this fundamental issue allows you to actually enjoy the process of paper piecing.

Save time by first cutting the fabric into squares or rectangles or cut the fabric to roughly echo the shape of the pattern pieces.

PATTERNS

My favorite pattern material for paper piecing is freezer paper. Some folks use regular paper, but I prefer the stability of pressing my pieces to the freezer paper. You can also see the reverse side easily through the freezer paper, which is crucial in ensuring adequate coverage of your fabric.

1. Trace the pattern on the dull/paper side of the freezer paper. Your design will be reversed, so make sure to account for this if you have a directional design, like a letter or any other asymmetrical design. Write the number of each piece.

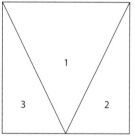

Trace pattern.

Piece by Numbers

For *Flags* (page 118), it doesn't matter which seam you sew first, as long as the center triangle is put in place first. For more complex paper piecing blocks, the order in which you sew matters, so make sure the pieces on the pattern are numbered according to the order in which each is to be sewn. This order ensures that the design will come out as intended. The line between consecutively numbered pieces is your seamline.

2. Cut out the pattern around the outside perimeter of the block. *Do not cut the individual pieces!* Do not worry about seam allowances on the pattern at this point. That comes with the sewing and trimming.

SEWING

1. Reduce your machine's stitch length to 14–18 stitches per inch.

2. Place the first piece of fabric (#1) on the pattern, with the *wrong side* of the fabric against the *shiny side* of the freezer paper. The fabric should entirely cover the #1 portion of the pattern, plus adequate seam allowance on all sides. Press lightly to hold it in place.

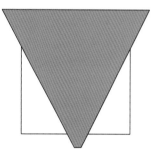

3. Cut a piece of fabric about ½˝ larger on all sides than the #2 pattern piece. It doesn't have to be the same shape as the pattern, as long as it is large enough. It's usually easier to just cut a square or rectangle.

4. Determine which edge will be stitched to piece #1 and fold the edge under ¼˝. Line up this folded edge with the seamline between pattern pieces #1 and #2, as if it was already sewn. The *wrong side* of the fabric should be against the *shiny side* of the freezer paper, covering section #2. This will confirm that the piece of fabric will cover the pattern piece completely.

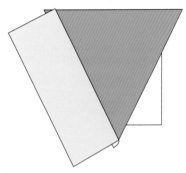

Fold edge to confirm coverage.

5. Holding on to the fabric at the seam-line, unfold it so the fabrics are right sides together. Hold the entire piece up to the light, still holding on to the fabric, to ensure that the fabric for piece #2 is still covering the seamline and that there is the appropriate seam allowance. The fold line in the fabric from Step 4 should be lined up with the seam-line on your pattern.

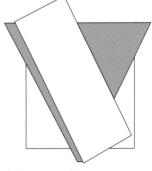

Position piece #2.

6. Turn the piece over to the *dull/paper side* and stitch on the seamline on your pattern.

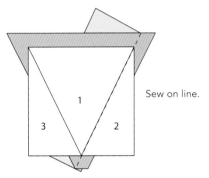

Sew on line.

7. Fold back the paper along the seamline so it is out of the way and trim the seam allow-ance to ¼˝. Press the seam flat; then unfold the pattern and press the seam and fabric.

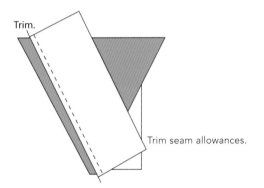

Trim.

Trim seam allowances.

8. Repeat Steps 3–7 for every pattern piece.

9. After you have sewn all the pieces, give the block a good press. Trim the outside edges of the blocks ¼˝ larger than the edge of your pattern piece; this is your seam allow-ance for joining blocks. Don't remove the paper yet. You will have edges that have some bias stretch to them, and keeping the paper on them reduces the potential for stretching with handling of the block. Remove the paper just before you sew all blocks together. A spritz of water helps when removing paper.

Chain Piecing

Having a dedicated sewing space with a large design wall is a luxury for many of us. In the real world, beds, the living room floor, and movable design walls are often called into use when laying out quilt tops. There is nothing wrong with any of that—but what if you haven't finished sewing the top together before your kids need to go to bed?

Chain piecing your blocks is the way to tackle this situation. You can arrange your quilt top, label the rows, and then pick it all up before you sew a stitch. Your blocks will stay in order, and you can work on piecing the top as time allows. This technique works when all blocks are the same size or when you are working on basic patchwork.

1. Arrange your quilt blocks by following piecing diagrams or dreaming up your own fantastic layout.

2. Using scraps of fabric or paper, create little labels numbered with the number of columns you have in your quilt. Gather these and an equal number of pins.

Grab Your Camera

Take a quick snapshot of your quilt layout before you start picking up the blocks. You never know who may move your blocks—errant children, big gusts of wind, or well-meaning partners. Even a cell phone photo will be enough to remind you of what your layout looked like so it can be re-created.

3. Pin the #1 label to the block in the top left corner. Working left to right, pin labels to the top block in each column.

4. Starting with the top left block, stack the entire column of blocks, keeping them in order from the top of the quilt to the bottom. Repeat with each column. You should now have stacks of blocks. If you aren't sewing them right away, put a pin or clip through each stack so they don't lose order. Make sure the label is on each stack.

5. When you are ready to sew, take the first 2 stacks to your sewing machine. Sew together the first 2 blocks from each stack. Do not cut the thread at the end of the seam. Sew a few stitches then join the next 2 blocks. Repeat this until you've sewn together all the blocks in those 2 stacks.

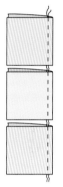

Chain piecing

6. Press the seams flat, then press to one side. Starting at the top, press to the right. Then press the second pair to the left. Alternate pressing directions down the column. When you alternate pressing directions, it is easier to line up your seams when you are sewing the rows together. If you prefer to press your seams open, feel free to do so.

7. Sew the blocks in the third stack to the joined blocks, chain piecing as before. Press in the same directions as you did in Step 6. Repeat sewing and pressing for all the stacks.

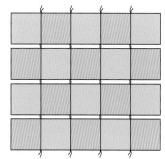
Sew stacks into rows.

8. All of your blocks should now be sewn together in rows. Yes, rows. Using this method of stacking the blocks into columns actually creates rows. Start in the middle as you pin and sew together the rows. If you pressed in alternate directions, your seams should nest together nicely.

9. Press seams to one side or open. Repeat sewing together the rows and pressing. If you press to one side, I recommend pressing all the seams in one direction.

Now the top is done!

> ### Create Dedicated Labeling Pieces
> Cut twenty light-colored scraps roughly 1″ × 1″. Number the scraps with a fabric pen or marker. Keep them together in a little bag or box to pull out when you need to piece a quilt top. Cut more if needed.

Finishing Touches

Quite often the details matter more than the overall design. All the projects in this book are designed to be used. That means you are going to touch them, see them, and use them at close range. The little finishing details might seem nitpicky, but taking the time to do them right will make all the difference to your final product.

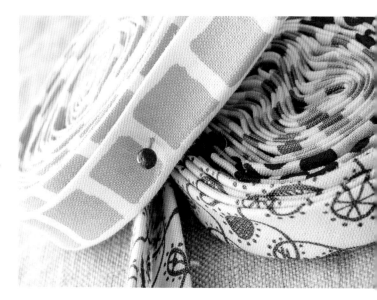

BIAS STRIPS

Ask a group of quilters about binding, and a heated debate about the merits of bias binding versus straight-grain binding ensues. Regardless of where you side on the debate, knowing how to create bias strips is a handy technique to have in your repertoire. Bias strips can be used for more than binding quilts. And they come in handy, quite a lot, when you are binding something that has curved edges.

Bias strips are strips cut on the diagonal of the fabric. The bias of the fabric is much stretchier than the fabric's straight or cross grain, which allows the bias strip to move around curves and irregular edges with greater ease. Bias strips are also a great way to see a fabric in a new way, such as seeing stripes or plaids on the diagonal.

Cutting Bias Strips

1. Cut off the selvages and press the fabric to remove any creases. Fold over an edge at a 45° angle to make a square. Cut off just the edge of the fold. Figure A

2. Carefully move the cut triangle to the other end of the fabric. Sew the straight edges together, right sides together, to create a parallelogram. Press the seam open. Figure B

3. Use a long ruler to measure and cut strips the desired width. Figure C

4. Sew together the strips by placing them right sides together and perpendicular to each other at one end. Sew them together on a 45° angle. Trim and press. Figure D

5. Fold and press in half lengthwise to make a double-layer binding. For a single-layer binding, see Binding Tape (page 140).

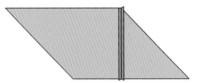

A. Cut off 45° triangle.

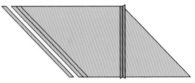

B. Create parallelogram.

C. Cut strips.

D. Sew together strips with diagonal seam.

Save Your Leftover Bias Strips

Sew your leftover bias strips together, mixing up the colors and patterns, to make ribbons or ties that are perfect for wrapping quilts when you give one as a gift. Or use them for the Napkins with Built-In Ties (page 73) or the Parade Pennants (page 42)!

How Much Fabric Do You Need to Make Bias Strips?

Use the following chart to determine how much fabric you need.

STEP	EXAMPLE: Make 2½˝ bias binding strips for a 36˝ × 54˝ quilt.
1. Add together the length of all sides of your project.	36 + 36 + 54 + 54 = 180
2. Add 10˝ to this number.	180 + 10 = 190
3. Multiply this number by the width of the binding strip you want.	190 × 2.5 = 475
4. Take the square root of that number.	$\sqrt{475} = 21.8$
5. This equals the length of piece you need for cutting your bias strips. I generally add a couple of inches and round up, just for a bit extra.	If you don't want a lot of leftovers, you should start with this length for each side of the square to make your bias strips. Round to the nearest inch.

BINDING TAPE

You can buy bias binding tape in various widths and tones of colors at the fabric store. *Or*, for the price of one package, more or less, you can buy a bias tape maker and make your own tape with your fabric of choice. You can create binding tape with bias strips or on-grain strips. Then you can use the binding tape on anything from quilts to napkins (page 73) to fun projects such as the Parade Pennants (page 42).

My favorite tool for creating binding tape is the Clover Bias Tape Maker. It comes in many sizes, from ¼˝ to 2˝. The size indicates the measurement for the final width of the bias tape. I like the ¼˝ and ½˝ sizes. If you make a lot of bias tape, there is also an electric version available that folds and presses for you.

To make the tape, cut strips of fabric the appropriate width, run them through the tool, and press well as it comes out the other end. That's it.

You can also make single-layer binding tape without any tools, other than your iron. Simply fold the strip in half, wrong sides together, and press. Then open up and fold the edges in toward the center fold and press again. Just watch your fingers as you do this—irons are hot!

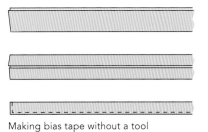

Making bias tape without a tool

SEWING BINDING TO A QUILT

Binding a quilt is like adding sprinkles to a cake. Sure, you could serve the cake without them, or simply turn the quilt edges with a pillowcase fold, but it will look so much more exciting with that extra dash of color.

Note: If you are using double-layer binding, leave the strips folded and sew both raw edges to the quilt. If you are using single-layer binding tape, open the folds and sew a single layer to the quilt or project.

1. Starting about 6″ from a corner, pin the binding on one side of the quilt, leaving about 3″ unattached. Sew on the binding with a ¼″ seam allowance.

2. Stop ¼″ from the corner. Backstitch and lift your needle. Fold the binding up so the fold forms a 45° angle. Fold the binding down and align it with the edge of the quilt.

3. Start stitching ¼″ from the edge and sew the next edge. Repeat at each corner. Stop sewing about 4″ from where you started. Backstitch.

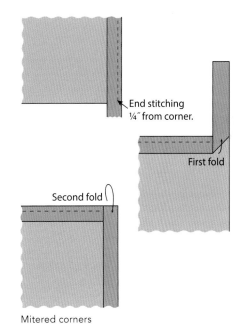

End stitching ¼″ from corner.

First fold

Second fold

Mitered corners

4. Join the ends (see Finishing Binding Ends on page 142). Finish sewing the binding to the quilt. Bring the folded edge to the back and stitch in place.

FINISHING BINDING ENDS

1. Fold the ending tail of the binding back on itself where it meets the beginning binding tail.

2. From the fold, measure and mark the cut width of your binding strip. Cut the ending binding tail to this measurement. For example, if the binding is cut 2⅛″ wide, measure from the fold on the ending tail of the binding 2⅛″ and cut the binding tail to this length.

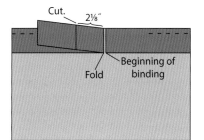

Cut binding tail.

3. Open both tails. Place one tail on top of the other at right angles, right sides together.

4. Mark a diagonal line from corner to corner and stitch on the line.

5. Check that you've done it correctly and that the binding fits the quilt; then trim the seam allowance to ¼″. Press open.

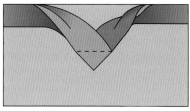

Stitch ends of binding diagonally.

Need More Information?

For more information on any of the techniques mentioned in the patterns and not described here, I suggest referring to the books below. I encourage you to explore new techniques and push your creativity. If you feel challenged by any of the techniques, that isn't necessarily a bad thing—it's just a reason to stop, breathe, and plunge into something new. Sewing is supposed to be relaxing, not stressful. Just like a Sunday afternoon.

Modern Quilts, Traditional Inspiration, by Denyse Schmidt, STC Craft / A Melanie Falick Book, 2012

The Practical Guide to Patchwork: New Basics for the Modern Quiltmaker, by Elizabeth Hartman, Stash Books, 2010

Sunday Morning Quilts: Sort, Store, and Use Every Last Bit of Your Treasure, by Amanda Jean Nyberg and Cheryl Arkison, Stash Books, 2012

About the Author

Answers

from page 62

Across

1. Giggles
2. Sunshine
3. Breathe
4. Nap
5. Respite
6. Teatime
7. Chillax

Down

1. Linger
2. Sleep in
3. Relaxation
4. Brunch
5. Eat
6. Walks

When Cheryl was a kid, her family bet her ten dollars that she couldn't keep silent for an entire family meal. It was the easiest money her family won. Cheryl never stops talking, let alone writing, designing, or cooking. This means she never stops creating.

As a mother to three kids who have only two modes—awake and asleep—it also means she simply never stops. It might be her Ukrainian heritage and the work ethic that comes with it, or perhaps it is simply a matter of there always being something fun to do. In the midst of full-time motherhood, Cheryl finds time to write books, teach quilting, and maintain a small freelance writing career.

Calgary, Alberta, is home for Cheryl, who lives with her wickedly handsome and sarcastic husband; two gregarious girls with enough wit, charm, and energy to feed a village; and one little boy who is happy to take in the day with eyes wide open. Her perfect day starts with tea and the family (wrestling match optional). Most likely it ends with a cocktail (gin in the summer and scotch in the winter) and conversation. And somewhere in there she will quilt.

Also by Cheryl Arkison, with Amanda Jean Nyberg

stash BOOKS ®

fabric arts for a handmade lifestyle

If you're craving beautiful authenticity in a time of mass-production...Stash Books is for you. Stash Books is a line of how-to books celebrating fabric arts for a handmade lifestyle. Backed by C&T Publishing's solid reputation for quality, Stash Books will inspire you with contemporary designs, clear and simple instructions, and engaging photography.

www.stashbooks.com